52
67
75
81
122
152
92/?
93/

Mama Cooks
FOR CHRISTMAS

by Toni Reifel and Bette Woodward

Editor - Judy Mackel

Cover and Graphics - Suzanne Jamieson

Additional copies may be obtained by addressing:

MAMA COOKS FOR CHRISTMAS
P.O. Box 7991
Newport Beach, 92658

Quantity copies of Mama Cooks for Christmas may be obtained for fundraising projects or by retail outlets at special discount rates. Please write for further information.

Have you tried our first cookbook, Mama Cooks A Day Ahead? This book has twice as many recipes and we know you will enjoy all the old favorites. Price is $14.95 plus tax and may be purchased from the same above address.

Copyright © 1991

ISBN   0-9628049-2-4

Toni Reifel
Bette Woodward

Newport Beach, California

Bookcrafters, Inc.

- INTRODUCTION -

Dear Friends,

    Thinking about Christmas, our mind's eye often drifts to the kitchen where we can vision marvelous recipes coming alive and the delightful smells of the holiday season.

Mama Cooks For Christmas,

is just this kind of book. We have gathered a treasure of recipes in hopes our special moments with family and friends will add to your special occasions. Wonderful stuffings and sauces abound, including decorative salads and scrumptious dishes no one can resist.

    It is with joy we share our very special recipes with you.

    Enjoy,

Toni Reifel   - -   Bette Woodward

MAMA COOKS FOR CHRISTMAS

TABLE OF CONTENTS

CHRISTMAS APPETIZERS	1 - 12
CHRISTMAS BEVERAGES	13 - 24
CHRISTMAS BRUNCH & BREADS	25 - 38
CHRISTMAS COOKIES & CANDIES	39 - 70
CHRISTMAS SALADS	71 - 82
CHRISTMAS MENUS	83 - 90
CHRISTMAS MAIN DISHES	91 - 103
CHRISTMAS SIDE DISHES & STUFFING	105 - 120
CHRISTMAS VEGETABLES	121 - 134
CHRISTMAS DESSERTS	135 - 163

Christmas Appetizers

CHRISTMAS APPETIZERS

BROCCOLI DIP

1	pkg. frozen chopped broccoli, cooked and drained
2	eggs, hard cooked and chopped
1/4	Cup Best Foods mayonnaise
3	Tbsp. Parmesan cheese, grated
1	Tbsp. fresh lemon juice
1	Tbsp. mustard
1/2	tsp. salt
1/2	Tbsp. pepper

In a food processor add all ingredients. Mix well. Store in a covered container overnight in the refrigerator.

WHEN READY TO SERVE - Serve as a dip with cut vegetables or with crackers.

VARIATION: Wonderful when served as a topping for a baked potato.

CHRISTMAS APPETIZERS

SHERRY CHEESE PATÉ

2	(3 oz.) pkgs. cream cheese, softened
4	tsp. sherry
1/2	tsp. curry powder
1	Cup cheddar cheese, shredded
1	(8 oz.) jar mango chutney
2	green onions, finely sliced

In a mixing bowl, cream together cream cheese, sherry and curry powder. Gradually add cheese and mix well. Spread into a lighty oiled mold and refrigerate overnight.

WHEN READY TO SERVE - Unmold and place on serving dish. Top with chutney and garnish with green onions. Serve with an assortment of crackers.

CHRISTMAS APPETIZERS

CHICKEN PATÉ

For a holiday Open House

1	whole chicken
1	Cup chicken stock
1	onion, chopped
2	tsp. salt
2	eggs, hard cooked
	Juice of 1/2 lemon
1	Tbsp. Worcestershire sauce
1	Tbsp. butter
2	green onions, chopped
	Salt and pepper to taste

Place chicken in saucepan. Cover with water. Add onion and salt. Boil until meat falls off bone. Remove from heat. Reserve strained liquid and place in refrigerator to allow fat to surface.

Discard chicken skin and bones. Place chicken meat into food processor. After degreasing chicken stock add 1 cup to processor. Add hard cooked eggs and remaining ingredients to food processor. With on and off motion chop until it forms a ball.

Press into covered container and refrigerate overnight.

WHEN READY TO SERVE: Serve on toast rounds.

CHRISTMAS APPETIZERS

MARINATED CHICKEN WINGS

```
25      chicken wings
2/3     Cup soy sauce
3       Tbsp. honey
1       clove garlic, minced or
            1 tsp. garlic juice
1/2     Cup pineapple juice
```

Discard wing tips. Split chicken wings at joint. Combine remaining ingredients and pour over chicken wings. Cover and store in refrigerator overnight.

In a baking dish, place marinated chicken wings in a single layer. Bake for 1 hour at 350°. Turn occasionally so the browning is even.

May be made in advance and frozen. Reheat at 250°.

CHRISTMAS APPETIZERS

COMPANY CRAB MOUSSE

Serves 12

1	can cream of mushroom soup
1	(8 oz.) pkg. cream cheese, softened
1	envelope unflavored gelatin
1	(6 1/2 oz.) can crab meat, rinse and drain
1/2	Cup cooked shrimp, cut into small pieces
1	Cup celery, diced
1/2	Cup green onion, chopped
1	Tbsp. fresh lemon juice
1	tsp. Worcestershire sauce
1/4	tsp. seasoned salt
	Light cooking oil
	Parsley (garnish)

Lightly oil a 4 Cup mold. In a saucepan, over low heat, combine soup, cream cheese and gelatin - stir until smooth and creamy (about 1-2 minutes). Remove from heat - add remaining ingredients. Pour mixture into prepared mold. Cover and chill in refrigerator overnight.

WHEN READY TO SERVE - Remove from mold on to a bed of greens. Garnish with holiday colors; "green" parsley and "red" pimientos. Serve with an assortment of crackers.

CHRISTMAS APPETIZERS

DEVILED EGGS

Serves 6 - 8

6	eggs, hard cooked
	Juice of 1 lemon
1/2	Cup Best Foods mayonnaise
1	Tbsp. French's mustard
3	Tbsp. onion, finely grated
1	Tbsp. Worcestershire Sauce
3	sprigs parsley, minced
	Salt and pepper to taste

Parsley leaves and paprika for garnish

Hard cook eggs and peel. Place halved cooked egg yolks in a bowl. Cream yolks with mayonnaise, lemon juice, mustard and Worcestershire. Mix in remaining ingredients. If not creamy enough add more mayonnaise or sour cream to achieve correct consistency. Fill each egg white cavity with egg yolk mixture. Cover and place in refrigerator until ready to serve.

WHEN READY TO SERVE - Garnish with a dash of paprika and a parsley leaf.

VARIATION - Substitute sour cream for mayonnaise.

CHRISTMAS APPETIZERS

DEVILED HAM HOLIDAY PUFFS

Serves 32

CREAM PUFFS:

2/3	Cup water
1/3	Cup butter
2/3	Cup flour
3	eggs, beaten

Preheat oven to 400°. Bring to boil in a saucepan water and butter. Reduce heat to low, vigorously stir in flour and stir until mixture forms a ball. Remove from heat. Add eggs and beat until smooth.

Drop on ungreased cookie sheet, a rounded teaspoon of dough, 1 inch apart. Bake for 20 minutes, until puffed and golden. Cool and set aside.

FILLING:		
	3	Tbsp. butter or margarine
	8	eggs
	1/4	Cup milk
	1/3	Cup onion, minced
	1/3	Cup green pepper, minced
	1/3	Cup red pepper, minced or pimiento, well drained
	2	cans (4 1/2 oz.) deviled ham
	32	baked cream puffs

CHRISTMAS APPETIZERS

DEVILED HAM HOLIDAY PUFFS (cont.)

Heat butter or margarine in skillet. Mix together, eggs and milk. Pour into skillet. Add onion, green pepper and pimiento. Stir together until eggs are thickened, but moist. Remove from heat.

Cut tops off cream puffs, reserve tops. Fill 1/4 full with deviled ham, add egg mixture, replace top and serve immediately.

VARIATION - This recipe can be used for making larger cream puffs. For serving 8, this makes a lovely brunch dish. Garnish the top of each cream puff with a sprig of holly.

CHRISTMAS APPETIZERS

MARINATED MUSHROOMS

Makes 6 small jars

2	lb. button mushrooms
1/4	Cup fresh lemon juice
1	Tbsp. parsley, minced
2	Tbsp. onion, minced
2	Tbsp. pimiento, chopped
1	clove garlic, minced
1/2	tsp. sugar
1/2	tsp. salt
1/8	tsp. oregano
1/8	tsp. pepper
1/4	Cup water
1/4	Cup olive oil
1/2	Cup cider vinegar

Clean mushrooms and trim off stems. In a large sauce pan, cover mushrooms with cold water. Add lemon juice. Bring to boil. Reduce heat, simmer for 1 minute. Drain.

In a large bowl, combine remaining ingredients and mix with drained mushrooms. Pack in sterilized jars and seal. Store at least 24 hours in refrigerator.

WHEN READY TO SERVE - Drain off liquid and serve with toothpicks on a tray with assorted blanched vegetables.

CHRISTMAS APPETIZERS

SALMON PARTY LOG

1	(#1) can (2 cups) salmon, drained
1	(8 oz) pkg. cream cheese, softened
2	tsp. onion, grated
1	tsp. prepared horseradish
1	Tbsp. lemon juice
1/4	tsp. salt

GARNISH:
- 1/2 Cup pecans, chopped
- 3 Tbsp. parsley, minced
- 1 pkg. sliced almonds
- 1 Maraschino cherry

Flake well drained canned salmon. Remove bones and dark meat. Add cream cheese, onion, horseradish, lemon juice and salt. Mix well. Chill for several hours before forming into a log or the shape of a fish. Garnish with nuts and parsley. For a fish shape: use almonds for fish scales, a cherry for an eye and parsley for the tail.

WHEN READY TO SERVE: Serve with an assortment of crackers. Very festive.

CHRISTMAS APPETIZERS

MARINATED SHRIMP

                                Serves 6 - 8

```
1 1/2 lb. raw shrimp
1     qt. water, boiling and salted
3/4   Cup salad oil
1/4   Cup wine vinegar
1/4   tsp. salt
1/2   tsp. sugar
1/2   tsp. Worcestershire Sauce
2 - 4 drops Tabasco Sauce
```

In boiling water, cook shrimp for 5 minutes or until pink. Drain and de-vein.

In a bowl add remaining ingredients and mix well. Add shrimp. Chill in refrigerator until ready to serve.

Serve plain or with an avocado dip.

CHRISTMAS APPETIZERS

SPINACH DIP

Serves 8 - 10

2	(10 oz.) pkgs. frozen chopped spinach, well drained
1	Cup sour cream
1/2	Cup mayonnaise or salad dressing
1/2	bunch parsley, minced
1/2	onion, minced
1	tsp. salt
1/2	tsp. celery salt
1/4	tsp. pepper
1/8	tsp. nutmeg

Cherry tomatoes or pimiento slices (garnish)

Add to spinach, remaining ingredients and mix well. Cover and store in refrigerator overnight.

WHEN READY TO SERVE - Garnish with pimiento slices or halved cherry tomatoes. Serve with a variety of cut raw vegetables.

Christmas Beverages

CHRISTMAS BEVERAGES

CAPPUCCINO

Serves 2

4   tsp. instant coffee crystals
2   Cups prepared whipped cream
1   Cup boiling-hot milk

1/2   tsp. ground cinnamon or chocolate
       for garnish

In a blender, add instant coffee and 1 cup of whipped cream, blend well. At medium speed, add boiling-hot milk. Pour mixture into 6-oz. coffee cups. Top with remaining whipped cream.

GARNISH with ground cinnamon or chocolate.

VARIATION - Serve over ice. A delightful iced coffee.

CHRISTMAS BEVERAGES

CRANBERRY CORDIAL

4   Cups cranberries, coarsely ground
3   Cups sugar
2   Cups gin or vodka

In a large jar, mix together cranberries, sugar and liquor. Cover tightly. Everyday for 3 weeks, shake the jar very well. When time is up, strain through cheese cloth. Can be stored without refrigeration.

Strained off berries can be used for ice cream topping or in other baking recipes.

This makes a nice holiday hostess gift!

CHRISTMAS BEVERAGES

DOUBLE CHOCOLATE EGG NOG

Serves 25 - 30

6	eggs
1/2	Cup sugar
4	Cups chocolate milk
1	tsp. vanilla
1/4	tsp. nutmeg
3	Cups whipped cream
3	Cups chocolate ice cream, softened

Ground Nutmeg
Chocolate curls

Beat eggs until frothy. Beating at high speed, gradually add sugar (about 5 minutes) or until mixture is very thick. Stir in milk, vanilla and nutmeg. Pour mixture into large container. Gently fold in ice cream and 2 Cups whipped cream. Store in refrigerator until ready to serve.

WHEN READY TO SERVE - Pour into large bowl and top with remaining whipped cream. Garnish with nutmeg and chocolate curls.

CHRISTMAS BEVERAGES

OLD FASHIONED EGG NOG

    For a Tree Trimming Party!

12	eggs, separated
1	Cup sugar
1	Cup brandy
2	Cups whiskey
2	qts. cream
	Grated nutmeg

Beat egg yolks until light. Gradually add sugar to beaten egg yolks. Add brandy, whiskey and cream. Beat egg whites until frothy and gently fold in.

WHEN READY TO SERVE - Sprinkle cup of egg nog with grated nutmeg.

CHRISTMAS BEVERAGES

CHRISTMAS SPICED GLOGG

Serves 10

30	whole cloves
3	whole oranges, unpeeled
1	Tbsp. lemon juice
2	qts. apple cider or apple juice
10	cinnamon sticks for garnish

Press 10 cloves into each orange and bake in 350° oven for 30 minutes. Set aside.

On top of stove, heat apple cider or juice until bubbly. Remove from heat; stir in lemon juice.

Before placing in a heat proofed punch bowl, pierce each orange with several holes with an ice pick. Add warm apple juice and serve immediately.

GARNISH each cup with a cinnamon stick.

VARIATION - This recipe is also delicious using 1 quart cider, and 1 quart cranberry juice.

CHRISTMAS BEVERAGES

IRISH CREAM

Makes 1 fifth

1	Cup whiskey
1	Tbsp. instant coffee
1	Tbsp. chocolate syrup
1	can Eagle Brand milk
1	Cup whipped cream
3	eggs

In a blender, mix all the ingredients together. Pour into a sealed container and store in refrigerator.

Serve in liqueur glasses, or give as a hostess gift in a decorative container.

CHRISTMAS BEVERAGES

KAHLUA

4	Cups sugar
2	Cups water
2	oz. instant coffee, powdered
1	fifth brandy
1	vanilla bean

In a sauce pan, heat sugar with 1 1/2 cups water. Stir until dissolved.

Break the vanilla bean and place in the bottom of a 1 1/2 gallon container. Add 1/2 cup boiling water. Stir in coffee and mix until dissolved. Add brandy. Add heated sugar water. Mix well. Secure top and let stand for one month.

A thoughtful Christmas gift.

CHRISTMAS BEVERAGES

HOLIDAY MIMOSAS

Serves 6

1   small can frozen orange juice
3   Tbsp. sugar
2 to 3 Tbsp. Eagle Brand milk
2   juice cans of water

1   bottle Champagne

Excluding champagne, add all ingredients to blender and blend until frothy.

WHEN READY TO SERVE - Fill each stemmed glass half full with juice mixture and top with champagne.

CHRISTMAS BEVERAGES

CHRISTMAS PUNCH

Serves 50

1	(12 oz.) can concentrated frozen orange juice, prepared according to package
1	(6 oz.) can concentrated frozen lemonade, prepared according to package
2 1/2	Cups (#2 can) pineapple juice
1 1/2	qts. water
6	pints cranberry juice cocktail *3 qts / 96 oz?*
6	Tbsp. sugar
1	orange, thinly sliced for garnish
1	lemon, thinly sliced for garnish

Mix all ingredients together and pour over crushed ice or ice cubes into a large punch bowl.

GARNISH with orange and lemon slices.

CHRISTMAS BEVERAGES

RASPBERRY CHAMPAGNE PUNCH

2	pkgs. frozen red raspberries in syrup, thawed
1/3	Cup lemon juice
1/2	Cup sugar
1	qt. raspberry sherbert
1	bottle rose wine, chilled
1	bottle champagne

In a blender, puree raspberries. Pour into punch bowl. Add lemon juice, sugar and wine. Stir until sugar dissolves. Keep chilled until ready to serve.

WHEN READY TO SERVE - Add sherbert and champagne. Gently mix together.

CHRISTMAS BEVERAGES

HOT BUTTERED RUM

To warm you after caroling!

1	qt. vanilla ice cream
1	lb. butter
1	lb. powdered sugar
1	lb. brown sugar
1	tsp. cinnamon
1/2	tsp. nutmeg

Rum

Excluding rum, mix all ingredients together, cover and store in the freezer until ready to serve.

WHEN READY TO SERVE - Place 1 heaping teaspoon of mixture into the bottom of cup or mug. Add one jigger of rum. Mix together. Add boiling water to top of cup. Gently stir each cup before adding garnish.

GARNISH with a dash of nutmeg and a cinnamon stick.

VARIATION - Substitute brandy for rum.

CHRISTMAS BEVERAGES

TOM AND JERRY

The secret to this recipe is a stiff batter and serving in a warm mug.

BATTER: 1   egg, separated
                    confectioners sugar
             1   pinch baking soda
             1/4   oz. rum

Beat the egg yolk separate from the egg white. Beat the egg white until stiff and combine. Add enough sugar to stiffen the mixture. Add rum and mix together. Add enough sugar to stiffen the mixture again. Cover and set aside.

WHEN READY TO SERVE - In the bottom of a cup, add 1 tablespoon batter mixture. Add 3 tablespoons hot milk and 1 1/2 oz. rum. Mix well. Fill each cup with hot milk and gently stir. Garnish with a dash of nutmeg.

Serve this on a cold night when guests drop in.

Christmas Brunch and Breads

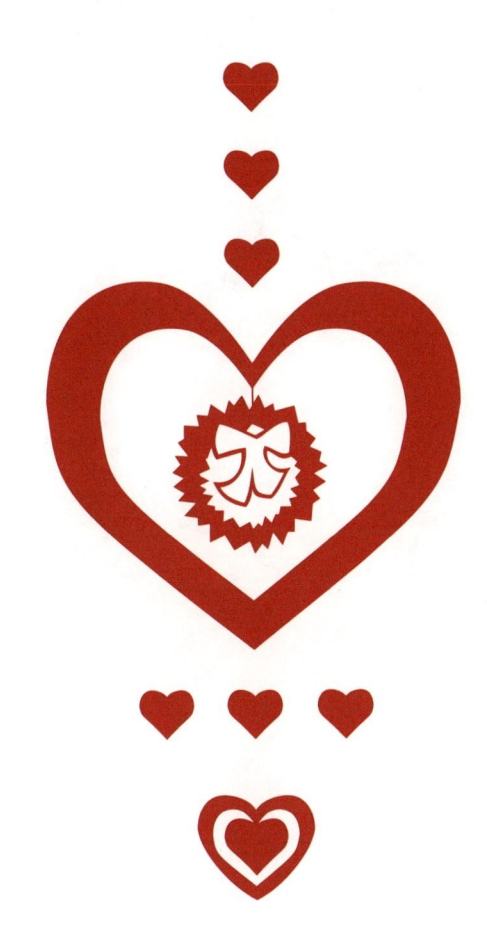

CHRISTMAS BRUNCH & BREADS

SAUTEED APPLES WITH NOODLES AND SAUSAGE

Serves 6 - 8

3	large Golden Delicious apples, unpeeled, cored and sliced thick
3	Tbsp. butter, melted
1	tsp. sugar
1/2	lb. noodles, cooked and drained
1/2	lb. sausage, cooked and crumbled

In a wide frying pan, melt butter and add apples. Cook over moderate high heat, gently turning from time to time. Sprinkle with sugar, when fruit begins to soften and is slightly browned. Cook for 1 minute before removing from heat to add cooked noodles and sausage. Place in a buttered casserole, cover and chill in refrigerator overnight.

WHEN READY TO SERVE - Heat uncovered in a 325° oven for 10 minutes.

Excellent Christmas brunch dish.

CHRISTMAS BRUNCH & BREADS

CHRISTMAS CAKE (JOLAKAKA)

Makes 2 loaves

1/2	Cup shortening
1 1/2	Cups sugar
3	eggs
3	Cups flour
3	tsp. baking powder
1/2	tsp. salt
1/4	tsp. cardamom
1	Cup raisins
1/2	Cup citron, chopped
1	Cup milk

Cream shortening, sugar and eggs together. Sift flour, baking powder and salt. Add alternately with milk to the creamed mixture. Add cardamom, raisins and citron. Bake in 2 greased loaf pans in a 350° oven for 1 hour.

CHRISTMAS BRUNCH & BREADS

PARTY COFFEE CAKE

3   Cups flour
1 1/2   tsp. baking soda
1 1/2   tsp. baking powder
1/4   tsp. salt
1/2   Cup butter, softened
        to room temperature
1/4   Cup sugar
3   large eggs
1/4   Cup bourbon
2   Cups sour cream
3/4   Cup brown sugar
1   Cup pecans, finely chopped
1   tsp. cinnamon

Sift together flour, baking soda, baking powder and salt. Cream butter with white sugar. Add eggs, one beaten egg at a time. Between each egg addition beat batter for 1 minute. Mix bourbon with sour cream. Add to butter mixture. Gradually combine dry ingredients with creamy mixture until well blended. Set aside. In a separate bowl, mix together brown sugar, nuts and cinnamon.

In a greased 9" tube pan pour in a layer of batter. Top with half of brown sugar mixture. Repeat with another layer of batter and top with remaining brown sugar mixture. Bake at 375° for 55-60 minutes in lower third of oven. Cool 10 minutes before inverting pan onto plate.

CHRISTMAS BRUNCH & BREADS

CRANBERRY BREAD

Makes 1 loaf

2	Cups flour
1/2	Cup sugar
1	Tbsp. baking powder
1/2	tsp. salt
2/3	Cup fresh orange juice
2	eggs, beaten slightly
3	Tbsp. sweet butter, melted
1/2	Cup coarsely chopped nuts
1 1/2	Cups cranberries
2	tsp. grated orange rind

Preheat oven to 350°. Grease loaf pan.

Sift flour, sugar, baking powder and salt into a mixing bowl. Make a well in the middle of the sifted mixture and pour in orange juice, eggs and melted butter. Mix well, but don't over mix. Fold in nuts, cranberries and orange rind.

Pour batter in pan and rest on middle rack of oven. Bake 45-50 minutes @ 350° or until knife inserted comes out clean. Cool in pan for 10 minutes...remove from pan and cool completely on rack.

Wrap in foil or put in plastic bag for 1-2 days before serving.

This bread is an especially nice gift during the holidays.

CHRISTMAS BRUNCH & BREADS

HAWAIIAN BREAD

Makes 3 medium loaves

4	Cups flour
1	tsp. soda
1	tsp. salt
1 1/2	Cup sugar
4	eggs, well beaten
1	(2 1/2 oz.) can undrained crushed pineapple
1	(8 oz.) pkg. coconut flakes

Sift flour and soda together. Add sugar. Add eggs and mix well. Add pineapple and coconut and mix until well blended.

Divide dough into thirds. Place each division into a well greased and floured loaf pan. The pan should be 1/2 full. Bake at 350° for 1 hour.

CHRISTMAS BRUNCH & BREADS

SOUR CREAM NUT BREAD

                              1 large loaf pan

1	pint sour cream
2	Cups flour
1	tsp. salt
3/4	tsp. soda
1	egg, beaten
1	Cup brown sugar
3/4	Cup walnuts, chopped

Sift together flour, soda and salt. Mix together egg, brown sugar and sour cream. Blend together and stir until smooth. Add nuts. Pour into a well greased loaf pan and bake in a 350° oven for 1 hour. Allow to cool on a rack.

CHRISTMAS BRUNCH & BREADS

HONEY PUFF PANCAKE

Serves 6

1	Cup milk
6	eggs
3	Tbsp. honey
1	3 oz. cream cheese
1	Cup flour
1/2	tsp. salt
1/2	tsp. baking powder
3	Tbsp. butter

Powdered sugar

Preheat oven to 400°. In blender add all ingredients except butter and sugar. Blend until frothy. Stop blender to scrape sides. Blend again for another minute. Let stand while butter melts in skillet.

When butter is bubbly remove skillet from cooktop. Pour egg mixture slowly into hot pan. Bake in oven at 325° until egg mixture puffs and is golden brown, (approx. 20 to 25 minutes). Serve immediately.

GARNISH with sprinkled powdered sugar. Serve with jam and lemon wedges. Delicious.

CHRISTMAS BRUNCH & BREADS

SWEDISH PANCAKES

Makes 6 - 8

1/2   cup flour
1   Tbsp. sugar
        Pinch of salt
2   eggs, beaten
1 1/2   Cups milk

Sift together flour, sugar and salt. Set aside. Beat eggs with milk. Add dry ingredients and beat until smooth. Cover and chill batter overnight.

WHEN READY TO SERVE - Beat batter again until smooth. Bake on a hot, lightly greased griddle. Serve with preserves.

CHRISTMAS BRUNCH & BREADS

PUMPKIN BREAD

Makes 3 loaves

```
2 2/3  Cups sugar
2/3    Cup shortening
4      eggs
1      (1 lb.) can pumpkin
2/3    Cup water
1/2    tsp. baking powder
2      tsp. baking soda
1      tsp. salt
1      tsp. cinnamon
1/2    tsp. ground cloves
2/3    Cup walnuts, chopped
2/3    Cup dates, chopped
3 1/4  Cups flour
```

Cream sugar and shortening. Add eggs, pumpkin and water. Sift together dry ingredients and add gradually to mixture. Mix well. Add dates and nuts. Mix until well blended.

Divide into 3 loaves and place into well greased and floured baking pans (should be 1/2 full). Bake in 350° oven for 1 hour and 15 minutes.

Keeps well and can be frozen.

VARIATION: Add 2/3 Cups raisins.

CHRISTMAS BRUNCH & BREADS

HERBED SPINACH QUICHE

Serves 4 - 6

2	Cups ham, diced
2	(10 oz.) pkgs. frozen spinach, cooked and drained
2	Cups rice, cooked
2	Cups cheddar cheese, grated
4	eggs, slightly beaten
4	Tbsp. butter or margarine, soften
2/3	Cup milk
4	Tbsp. onion, chopped
1	tsp. Worcestershire sauce
1	tsp. salt
1/2	tsp. Rosemary, crushed

Combine all ingredients and pour into a buttered 9" x 13" pan. Cover and refrigerate overnight.

WHEN READY TO SERVE - Let stand at room temperature for 20 minutes before baking for 40-45 minutes in a 350° oven or until knife inserted in center comes out clean. Sprinkle a little extra cheese on top and return to oven for 5 minutes.

Excellent for appetizer. Cut into small squares to serve 12. The recipe can be halved and baked in a pie shell.

This is a very popular brunch dish!

CHRISTMAS BRUNCH & BREADS

SAINT LUCIA BUNS
A Swedish Christmas tradition

1	pkg. dry yeast
1/4	Cup warm water
1/2	Cup butter
1	Cup light cream
1/2	Cup sugar
1/2	tsp. salt
1/4	tsp. thread saffron
2	eggs, beaten separately
4	Cups flour
	Course sugar
	raisins

Dissolve yeast in warm water. Set aside. Melt butter, stir in light cream. Pour lukewarm mixture over dissolved yeast. Stir in sugar, salt, crushed saffron and 1 egg. Add flour. Do not knead. Place contents in large, greased bowl. Cover, let rise for 1/2 an hour. On a lightly floured surface knead for 5 minutes or until smooth and shiny. Divide into 20 pieces and shape each into 10" ropes. Twist each rope into an "S" shape, coiling the ends into a snail fashion. Place 2" apart on a lightly greased baking sheet. Cover, let rise for 1 1/2 hours. Brush buns with remaining beaten egg, sprinkle with coarse sugar. Insert a raisin into the center of each "S" curl. Bake at 400° for 10-20 minutes or until golden brown.

CHRISTMAS BRUNCH & BREADS

SCONES

                                          Makes 1 dozen

2	Cups self-rising flour
1/2	tsp. salt
1	tsp. sugar
1/4	Cup butter
3/4	Cup combination of water and milk

TOPPING: Devonshire cream
                    Whipped jam

Sift flour and salt together. Add sugar. Add butter and fork together until dough resembles bread crumbs. Add enough water and milk combination until mixture has texture of soft dough. Kneed on lightly floured surface. Pat out to approximately 3/4" thickness. Cut 2" rounds and place on greased cookie sheet. Glaze tops by lightly brushing on milk. Bake in 400° oven for 10 minutes or until golden brown.

WHEN READY TO SERVE: Top with Devonshire cream and a dollop of jam.

VARIATION: Substitute buttermilk for milk. Add 1/4 Cup each of raisins and chopped dates.

CHRISTMAS BRUNCH & BREADS

CHILI-CHEESE STRATA

Serves 12

1	lb. white sandwich bread, crusts removed and cut into strips
1	onion, chopped finely
1	lb. sharp cheddar cheese, grated
1	can chopped green chilies
1	small jar sliced pimientos
4	eggs, beaten
3	Cups half and half
1	tsp. Worcestershire sauce
	Salt to taste

Combine eggs, milk, Worcestershire sauce and salt together. Set aside. In a buttered (8 1/2" x 11") casserole press bread into dish. Top with onion, cheese, pimientos and chilies. Cover with one half of egg mixture. Repeat bread layer, onion, cheese, pimientos and chilies. Add more egg mixture. Cover and chill in refrigerator overnight.

WHEN READY TO SERVE - Bake for 45 minutes in a 350° oven.

This is our favorite Christmas morning brunch dish!

CHRISTMAS BRUNCH & BREADS

ZUCCHINI BREAD

1 large loaf or 3 small tins

2	Cups zucchini, shredded
1	Cup white sugar
1	Cup brown sugar
3	Cups flour
1	tsp. salt
1	tsp. soda
1/4	tsp. baking powder
1	tsp. cinnamon
1	tsp. ground ginger
1	tsp. ground cloves
1	Cup oil
3	eggs, well beaten
3	tsp. vanilla
1/2	Cup nuts, chopped

Sift together sugars, flour, salt, soda, baking powder and spices. Add oil. Mix well. Add eggs. Mix until smooth. Add vanilla. Mix in zucchini and nuts. Place in well greased and floured loaf pans and bake for 45 minutes in a 325° oven.

Christmas Cookies and Candies

CHRISTMAS COOKIES & CANDIES

ALMOND CHRISTMAS COOKIES

Makes 2 dozen

1	Cup butter
1	Cup sugar
1	Cup ground almonds (unblanched)
2	Cups flour
1/2	tsp. salt
1	tsp. vanilla

Mix all ingredients together. On a floured board, pat dough to be 1/8" thick. With a small cookie cutter cut into attractive shapes.

Bake for 15 minutes in a 350° oven. While still warm, roll cookies in granulated sugar.

These cookies are delicious and will keep very well during the holidays when kept in a covered container.

CHRISTMAS COOKIES & CANDIES

ALMOND LACY COOKIES

Makes 7 dozen

2/3	Cups grated almonds (3 1/4 oz. package)
1/2	Cup butter
1/2	Cup sugar
2	Tbsp. milk
2	Tbsp. flour

In a sauce pan, combine all ingredients and heat until butter just melts.

For each cookie, spoon 1/2 tsp. warm batter onto a baking sheet covered with foil - - space 2 1/2" apart.

Bake for 6-7 minutes in a 350° oven. Allow cookies to cool on a cookie sheet for 10 minutes before removing cookies to a wire rack to cool completely.

These cookies are very fancy and lovely on a pretty Christmas plate.

CHRISTMAS COOKIES & CANDIES

ALMOND SQUARES

Makes 2 dozen

1/4	lb. butter
1/2	Cup sugar
1	egg yolk
1	Cup flour
1/4	tsp. cinnamon
1	Cup whole almonds, blanched
1	egg white, unbeaten

Mix all ingredients together. Wet your hands and press dough out onto a cookie sheet to be 1/8" thick. Place blanched almonds on top of dough and press gently into dough. Arrange almonds approximately 1" apart. Glaze with 1 unbeaten egg white. Bake for 1 hour at 250°. Cut while hot into squares and allow to cool.

This is a family recipe that we use every Christmas for serving or giving as gifts.

CHRISTMAS COOKIES & CANDIES

TERIYAKI ALMONDS

2	Cups blanched almonds
1/4	Cup butter or margarine
2	Tbsp. soy sauce
2	Tbsp. dry sherry
1/4 - 1/2 tsp. ground ginger
	Garlic salt to taste

Spread almonds on an ungreased cookie sheet. Toast for 20 minutes in a 300° oven. In a sauce pan, melt butter before adding soy sauce, sherry and ginger. Add toasted almonds and coat evenly. Spread nuts on an un-greased cookie sheet. In a 300° oven, toast coated nuts for 10 minutes, stirring occasionally. When toasted, remove from oven and add garlic salt to taste. Spread out on a paper bag. Before storing, allow to cool and dry.

Store covered tightly in the refrigerator or freezer.

Nice hostess gift.

CHRISTMAS COOKIES & CANDIES

HOLLY BOURBON BALLS

Makes 4 - 5 dozen

4	Cups graham crackers, crushed fine
4	Tbsp. cocoa
2	Cups confectioner's sugar, sifted
1/8	tsp. salt
2	Cups nuts, chopped
3	Tbsp. corn syrup
1/2	Cup bourbon or brandy

Combine above ingredients and thoroughly mix. Form into balls the size of a walnut. Roll in confectioner's sugar. Store in an air tight container and store for one week before serving.

VARIATION: Substitute crushed vanilla wafers for graham crackers. Add chopped raisins.

CHRISTMAS COOKIES & CANDIES

BUTTERBALLS

Makes 4 dozen

```
1       lb. butter
1       Cup powdered sugar
4 1/2   Cups flour
2       tsp. vanilla
2       Cups nuts, chopped
```

Mix all ingredients together and form into balls (about the size of a walnut).

Bake on an ungreased cookie sheet @ 300° for 45 minutes. Roll twice in powdered sugar and store in a covered container.

Make these cookies ahead to serve at Christmas or give as gifts.

CHRISTMAS COOKIES & CANDIES

CANDY CANE COOKIES

Making these with children is a memory long to hold dear

1	Cup shortening
1	Cup confectioners sugar, sifted
1	egg
1 1/2	tsp. almond extract
1	tsp. vanilla
1	Cup flour
1/2	tsp. red food coloring

Preheat oven to 375°. In a large bowl, mix shortening and sugar. Add egg, almond extract and vanilla. Sift in flour. Mix well.

Divide dough in half, placing each half in separate bowls. Mix food coloring into one bowl. On a floured board, break off about 1 tablespoon of each color dough. Roll by hand separately to 4" strips of each color. Place each color side by side and twist together. Form a candy cane when placing on an ungreased sheet. Bake in oven for 7 minutes.

CHRISTMAS COOKIES & CANDIES

CARAMELS

2	Cups sugar
1	Cup light corn syrup
1/2	Cup cream
3	Tbsp. butter
4	Tbsp. water
1/2	tsp. vanilla
1/2	Cup nuts, chopped

Mix together sugar, cream, syrup, butter and water. In a heavy pan, boil slowly until a hard ball forms when tested in cold water. Add vanilla and nuts. Pour into a buttered plate. Let stand until set. Cut into pieces before storing.

CHRISTMAS COOKIES & CANDIES

ENGLISH TOFFEE

2	Cups sugar
1	lb. butter
1	large Hershey's chocolate bar
1	Cup almonds, ground

In a heavy iron skillet, melt butter. While stirring constantly, add sugar to skillet and boil for 10 to 12 minutes. The mixture will turn a darker shade. Cook until little drops form a hard ball when placed on a saucer. Pour into a large flat pan or plate. Top with melted chocolate and nuts. When cool, break into pieces.

CHRISTMAS COOKIES & CANDIES

GRANDMA'S FUDGE

3	Cups semi sweet chocolate chips
1	can sweetened Eagle Brand milk
1 1/2	tsp. vanilla
1	Cup nuts, chopped
1 1/2	Cups mini marshmallows

In a heavy pan, melt chocolate chips. Add condensed milk and stir until smooth. Add vanilla, marshmallows and nuts and stir until blended.

Pour into a buttered pan, cover and place into refrigerator to cool. When cold, cut into squares.

CHRISTMAS COOKIES & CANDIES

GINGERBREAD PEOPLE

For your tree

2/3	Cup shortening
1/2	Cup brown sugar, packed
3/4	Cup light molasses
1	egg
3	Cups flour
1	tsp. baking soda
1/2	tsp. baking powder
2	tsp. ginger
1	tsp. cinnamon
1/4	tsp. ground cloves

Cream together shortening, brown sugar, molasses and egg. Sift dry ingredients together and add to creamed mixture. Stir well. Cover bowl and freeze for 20 minutes. Preheat oven to 375°. Roll dough to 1/8" thickness and with cookie cutter, cut gingerbread people. Bake for 8 - 10 minutes. Let cool and decorate.

When I make these cookies to be hung on the tree and to be given away to visiting guests, I make a small knife cut in the top of each cookie before baking. When cooled, I decorate their cute shapes and tie a bright colored ribbon before hanging.

CHRISTMAS COOKIES & CANDIES

CANDIED GRAPEFRUIT PEEL

A unique hostess gift!

4	grapefruit, halved
2	Cups sugar
1	Cup water

Granulated sugar

In a saucepan, cover grapefruit halves with cold water. Bring to boil and boil for 1/2 an hour. Remove from heat and scoop out insides. Cut rind into 1/4" thin strips.

In a saucepan, combine sugar and water. Boil until a thread forms when placed into cold water. When ready, add grapefruit rind strips and continue boiling until syrup is absorbed.

Remove from heat and roll candied rind in granulated sugar.

VARIATION - Lemon and orange peel could be substituted.

CHRISTMAS COOKIES & CANDIES

HOLIDAY DELIGHT

```
1/2     lb. Brazil nuts, coarsely chopped
1/2     lb. walnuts, coarsely chopped
1/2     lb. candied cherries, cut-up
1/2     lb. candied pineapple, cut-up
3       Cups sugar
1       Cup light corn syrup
1 1/3   Cup light cream
1 1/2   tsp. vanilla
```

Combine nuts and fruit. In a sauce pan, over medium heat, heat sugar, syrup and cream. Cook until soft ball stage. Remove from heat and beat until mixture thickens and changes color. Add vanilla. Beat again. Gradually stir in nuts and fruit. The mixture will be sticky.

In a wax paper lined, 8"x12" pan, press in mixture, using a wet spoon. Place in refrigerator for at least 24 hours. Remove from refrigerator to allow to dry-out. When dry, cut into squares and serve.

CHRISTMAS COOKIES & CANDIES

FRENCH LEMON SQUARES

1	egg
1	pkg. lemon cake mix
1/2	Cup margarine, softened

Mix together the above ingredients until crumbly. Set aside 1 cup of crumbled mixture. With remaining dough, lightly press into an ungreased baking pan (9" x 13"). Bake for 15 minutes in a 350° oven.

FILLING:
- 2 eggs
- 1 Cup sugar
- 1/2 tsp. baking powder
- 1/4 tsp. salt
- 2 tsp. lemon rind, grated
- 1/4 Cup lemon juice

Mix filling ingredients together and beat until light and foamy. Pour over hot baked cake. Sprinkle remaining crumbled mixture on top of cake. Bake for 15 minutes in a 375° oven. Sprinkle powdered sugar on top. Cool and cut into small squares.

CHRISTMAS COOKIES & CANDIES

LINZERTART

Makes 4 dozen

1/2	lb. margarine
1	Cup sugar
3	egg yolks, beaten
3	Cups flour
1	Cup pecans, chopped
	Raspberry jam

Cream margarine and sugar. Add egg yolks. Gradually add flour. Dough will be soft. Not taking the dough to the edge, press dough onto a buttered 10" x 15" jelly roll pan. Bake for 15 minutes or until light brown, in a 350° oven. Cool 5 minutes. Spread with raspberry jam, sprinkle with chopped pecans. While warm, cut in squares. When cool, remove from pan.

In a covered container, these treats store well.

CHRISTMAS COOKIES & CANDIES

MINCE MEAT MINIATURES

2	Cups quick rolled oats
2	Cups flour, sifted
1 1/3	Cup dark brown sugar, firmly packed
1 1/2	tsp. salt
1	tsp. cinnamon
1	Cup butter
1	(1 lb. 12 oz) jar brandied mince meat
1/2	Cup nuts, coarsely chopped

Excluding butter, mince meat and nuts, mix together all ingredients. Stir until well mixed. Cut in butter thoroughly. Add nuts. Mix well.

In a 9"x13" buttered glass pan spread 1/2 of the mixture and pat firmly. Spread mince meat on top. Add remaining dough. Bake for 1 hour in a 325° oven. Cool on a wire rack. Cut into squares. Cover and store in refrigerator until ready to serve.

CHRISTMAS COOKIES & CANDY

PEANUT BRITTLE

Makes 1 1/2 pounds

2	Cups sugar
2	Cups light corn syrup
1/2	Cup water
1/2	tsp. salt
3	Cups raw peanuts
2	Tbsp. butter
2	Tbsp. baking soda

In a heavy sauce pan, heat sugar, syrup, water and salt to a rolling boil. Add peanuts. Reduce heat to medium while stirring constantly. Cook until syrup spins a thread. Add butter. Then, add baking soda. Beat vigorously and pour on a buttered surface, spreading to 1/4" thickness. When cool break into pieces. Store in an airtight container.

CHRISTMAS COOKIES & CANDIES

PERSIMMON COOKIES

Makes 6 dozen

1/2	Cup butter
1	Cup sugar
1	egg
1	Cup persimmon pulp
2	Cups flour, sifted
1	tsp. soda
1/2	tsp. cinnamon
1/2	tsp. ground cloves
1/2	tsp. nutmeg
1	Cup dark raisins
1	Cup nuts, chopped

Preheat oven to 350°. Cream butter and sugar. Beat in egg and persimmon pulp. Stir vigorously until well blended. Add remaining ingredients. Mix well.

Drop by teaspoon on a greased cookie sheet. Bake for 12 - 15 minutes. Cool on a wire rack.

CHRISTMAS COOKIES & CANDIES

POPCORN BALLS

1	Cup sugar
1/2	Cup water
1	tsp. vinegar
2	Tbsp. light corn syrup
1/2	tsp. salt
1	Tbsp. butter
6	Cups popcorn, popped

Combine sugar, water, vinegar, syrup and salt. Cook to very hard stage (265°). Add butter. Remove from heat and pour over popcorn. Form into balls.

Wrap each popcorn ball in clear plastic wrap and tie with a holiday ribbon. See the children's surprise when peaking out of a Christmas stocking.

CHRISTMAS COOKIES & CANDIES

ROSETTES (Danish Christmas cookie)

Mix in order:

2	eggs, well beaten
1/4	tsp. salt
1	Tbsp. sugar
1	Cup flour
1	Cup milk

Powdered sugar

Dip hot Rosette iron in batter and fry in deep fat until crisp. Drain shells on paper towels.

Sprinkle with powdered sugar.

These Rosettes store well in covered containers and are "A Must" to serve at Christmas time.

CHRISTMAS COOKIES & CANDIES

SANTA'S COOKIES

                              Makes 5-6 dozen

CREAM:	1	Cup shortening
	4	Cups brown sugar
ADD AND MIX:	4	eggs, well beaten
	6	Cups flour (mixed with
	1	Tbsp. soda)
	1	tsp. vanilla

The dough will be stiff. Roll dough into logs, cover with plastic wrap and refrigerate overnight.

Slice and bake on greased cookie sheet in 350° oven for 10 minutes. Frost each cookie with thin frosting.

FROSTING:	1/2 lb. box powdered sugar
	1/4 cube soft butter
	1/2 Cup warm milk
	1 tsp. vanilla

Decorate with holly and red hots. Store in covered container.

These cookies are Santa's favorite.

CHRISTMAS COOKIES & CANDIES

CHRISTMAS STRAWBERRIES

1   (15 oz.) can Eagle Brand milk
2   (6 oz.) pkgs. strawberry Jello
1 1/2   Cups coconut, very fine
1   Cup vanilla wafers, finely crushed
        green sugar

In a bowl, combine the above ingredients. Cover and place in refrigerator overnight or at least until moisture has absorbed into dry ingredients.

The next day, or several hours later, form into 1" balls, and then work into the shape of a large strawberry. Press flat end of shaped strawberry into green sugar. Roll pointed sides into more dry strawberry jello. Wrap in clear plastic wrap until ready to serve.

Children love them! They brighten up a holiday table, when placed with the cookies and candies. Very festive.

CHRISTMAS COOKIES & CANDIES

SPRITZ COOKIES

                        Makes 4 - 5 dozen

```
1       Cup butter or margarine
1/4     tsp. salt
2/3     (generous) Cup sugar
3       egg yolks
1       tsp. vanilla
2 1/2   Cups sifted flour
1/2     tsp. baking powder
```

Cream shortening with salt, sugar and egg yolks. Beat well. Add vanilla. Combine baking powder and flour. Beat into mixture. Place mixture into a press of desired shape and squeeze out onto an ungreased cookie sheet. Bake for 10 -15 minutes in a 350° oven.

CHRISTMAS COOKIES & CANDIES

STARLIGHT SUGAR CRISPS

SIFT TOGETHER: 3 1/2 Cups flour
                 1 1/2 tsp. salt

1/2	Cup butter or margarine
1/2	Cup shortening
2	eggs, beaten
1/2	Cup sour cream
1	tsp. vanilla

Granulated sugar

SOFTEN: 1   pkg. dry yeast
                 1/4   Cup warm water

Cut butter and shortening into dry ingredients. Add eggs, sour cream and vanilla. Mix well. Add yeast mixture and mix well. Divide dough into 2 equal parts. Cover and chill for at least 2 hours in the refrigerator. (Dough will keep several days in the refrigerator.)

Roll each dough part on a sugar sprinkled surface in the form of a rectangle. Sprinkle with sugar and fold into thirds. Roll again and sprinkle with more sugar and repeat process twice more. Cut into strips and twist before baking on an ungreased cookie sheet for 15 - 20 minutes in a 375° oven.

CHRISTMAS COOKIES & CANDIES

SUGARPLUMS

Makes 1 1/2 dozen

18	(1 lb.) prunes, extra large
18	dates, pitted
18	dried apricots
3	Tbsp. peanut butter
	Granulated sugar

Place prunes in colander over boiling water. Cover and steam for 10 minutes, or until tender and plump. Remove from heat. Split lengthwise and remove pit from each prune.

Fill each pitted date with 1/2 tsp. peanut butter and enclose in an apricot half. Stuff each prune with a filled apricot-date. Push prune slit together, leaving a little apricot showing.

WHEN READY TO SERVE - Roll each stuffed prune in granulated sugar.

TO STORE: Place stuffed prunes in a tightly covered container. Keep refrigerated. Re-roll in sugar, when ready to serve again. Prunes keep for several weeks.

CHRISTMAS COOKIES & CANDIES

CHRISTMAS NUTS

1   lb. shelled pecan halves
1   Cup brown sugar
3 1/2 Tbsp. evaporated milk

Boil brown sugar and evaporated milk for 3 minutes and let stand for 10 minutes. Beat for 2-3 minutes. Mix with pecans. Separate and cool on waxed paper.

These are delicious to serve, or to put in containers and give as gifts.

CHRISTMAS COOKIES & CANDIES

CHOCOLATE TEA COOKIES

1	Cup brown sugar
1/2	Cup shortening
2	squares chocolate, melted
1	egg, slightly beaten
1/2	Cup milk
1 1/2	Cups flour
1/4	tsp. soda
1/2	tsp. salt
1/2	tsp. baking powder
1/2	Cup pecans, chopped
1/2	tsp. vanilla
	pecan halves

Cream sugar with shortening. Add melted chocolate. Add egg and milk. Add remaining dry ingredients and mix well. Add vanilla. Add nuts and mix together. Drop dough by the spoonful on a greased cookie sheet. Bake for 12 - 15 minutes in a 350° oven.

ICING:
- 1/4 Cup shortening
- 2 Cups powdered sugar
- 4 Tbsp. hot water
- 1/4 tsp. salt
- 1/2 tsp. vanilla
- 1 square chocolate, melted

CHRISTMAS COOKIES & CANDIES

CHOCOLATE TEA COOKIES (cont.)

Gradually add sugar, salt, vanilla and water to shortening. Mix together well. Set aside 1/3 of frosting mixture. To remaining mixture, add chocolate and 1 tsp. water. Mix well. Spread cookies with white frosting, then chocolate and top with pecan half.

My mother made these every Christmas to give to our family and friends.

CHRISTMAS COOKIES & CANDY

SPECIAL CHRISTMAS TEA COOKIES

Makes 5 dozen

2 1/4	Cup flour, sifted
1/2	tsp. salt
1	Cup powdered sugar
1	Cup butter, softened
1	egg, well beaten
2	tsp. vanilla
	Colored sugar
1/2	Cup nuts, chopped

Sift together flour, salt and sugar. Cut in butter until dough looks like coarse meal. Sprinkle on top of dough 2 Tbsp. of well beaten egg and vanilla. Blend well and roll dough out on a floured board to 1/8" thickness. Cut into desired shapes. Place cookies on an ungreased cookie sheet. Brush dough with remaining egg and sprinkle with colored sugar and/or nuts. Bake for 5 - 7 minutes in a 400° oven.

This is the easiest rolled cookie recipe I have ever used, and it is the best!

CHRISTMAS COOKIES & CANDIES

TRUFFLES

A chocolate lover's delight with a Schnapp!

1	Cup semi-sweet chocolate chips
1	Tbsp. butter, unsalted
1/4	Cup whipping cream
3	Tbsp. peppermint schnapps
3	Tbsp. unsweetened cocoa powder
2	Tbsp. confectioner's sugar

In a sauce pan, melt together chocolate chips and butter. Add cream and schnapps. Gently stir over moderate heat until smooth. Pour into a small ball. Cover and refrigerate until firm.

Sift together cocoa powder and sugar. Remove chocolate mixture from refrigerator and place bowl in ice water. Roll hardened chocolate into 1" balls. Coat chocolate balls by rolling in cocoa and sugar mixture. Cover and chill until ready to serve.

CHRISTMAS COOKIES & CANDIES

ORANGE SUGARED WALNUTS

A yummy Christmas treat!

1/2	Cup fresh orange juice
1	tsp. orange peel, grated
1	Cup sugar
1	tsp. cinnamon
1	tsp. salt

2 1/2 Cups walnut halves

Mix first five ingredients together. Place in a heavy pan and without stirring, cook mixture until candy thermometer reaches 236°. Add nuts and stir until creamy. Place separated nuts on a greased cookie sheet. Allow to cool.

Store in a sealed container.

CHRISTMAS COOKIES & CANDIES

WALNUT ROLL

1 1/2 quarts sugar
1   large &
1   small can evaporated milk
1   pint dark corn syrup
1   lb. walnuts, chopped
        Pinch of salt

Over a medium heat, heat sugar, milk and corn syrup. Cook until a solid ball forms when a sampling is placed in cold water. Add walnuts and stir until thick. Pour on oiled surface and knead (like bread) until a roll is formed. Cool. Wrap in plastic wrap and place in refrigerator. Slice when needed.

Small logs are lovely hostess gifts when wrapped in festive wrap and tied with ribbons.

Christmas Salads

CHRISTMAS SALADS

STAR BRIGHT ASPIC

1/2   Cup pimiento stuffed olives, sliced
1/4   Cup sharp cheese, grated
2   pkgs. lemon Jell-O

Dissolve Jell-O in 1 Cup boiling water.

2   (12 oz) cans V8 juice
1   Tbsp. vinegar
1   Tbsp. Worcestershire
      Few dashes of Tabasco
      Coarse ground pepper

Mix together and pour into a round tube mold that has been greased with mayonnaise.

GARNISH: 1   lb. cooked baby shrimp
              2   hard boiled eggs
                     Parsley sprigs

SAUCE: 1   Cup mayonnaise
              1/2   Cup ketchup
              1   Tbsp. lemon juice

Mix together.

CHRISTMAS SALADS

STAR BRIGHT ASPIC (cont.)

WHEN READY TO SERVE - Unmold and fill center of mold with cooked baby shrimp. Garnish with sliced eggs and parsley sprigs. Top with sauce.

This is a very nice dish to serve before a Christmas dinner or at a party buffet.

CHRISTMAS SALADS

PICKLED BEET SALAD

Serves 12 - 16

1   (3 oz.) pkg. strawberry Jell-O
1   (3 oz.) pkg. raspberry Jell-O
1   (3 oz.) pkg. cherry Jell-O

Dissolve in 4 Cups boiling water

1   (#305) can French cut beets, drain and save liquid
1/2   Cup sweet pickle juice
1   (#303) can crushed pineapple, drained

Add 1 cup combined pineapple and beet juice and 1/2 cup pickle juice to Jell-O mixture. Chill in refrigerator until syrupy. Stir in beets and pineapple. Pour into lightly oiled 3-quart mold or oiled 9"x13"x2" pan. Cover and chill overnight in refrigerator.

DRESSING:
1   Cup mayonnaise
1   Tbsp. green onion, minced
1   Tbsp. celery, finely chopped
1   Tbsp. green pepper, finely chopped

Mix all ingredients together. This is a delicious Christmas dinner salad.

CHRISTMAS SALADS

BROCCOLI SALAD

Serves 8

1 1/2 bunches fresh broccoli, chopped finely
10-12 slices crisp bacon, crumbled
1   Cup red seedless grapes
1   medium red onion, finely chopped

Mix broccoli and onions together, add grapes and bacon and toss.

DRESSING: 1   Cup mayonnaise
              1/4   Cup sugar
              2   Tbsp. vinegar

Pour over salad and stir.

With all its "red" and "green" it looks so pretty on the Christmas table!

CHRISTMAS SALADS

CHRISTMAS JELL-O MOLD

Serves 16 -20

1   pkg. strawberry Jell-O
1 1/4 cups water, boiling
1   can whole cranberry sauce

Dissolve Jell-O in boiling water. Add cranberry sauce. Pour into a lightly oiled 8 Cup Christmas mold. Chill until firm.

1   pkg. lemon Jell-O
1 1/4 Cup water, boiling
1   (8 oz.) pkg. cream cheese, softened
1   (9 oz) can crushed pineapple, drained
1/4   Cup salted pecans, chopped

Dissolve Jell-O in boiling water. Cool until mixture is syrupy. Whip in cream cheese, pineapple and nuts. Pour over firm cranberry layer. Chill until set firm.

1   pkg. lime Jell-O
1 1/4 Cup water, boiling
1   (1 lb.) can grapefruit sections with juice

CHRISTMAS SALADS

CHRISTMAS JELL-O MOLD (cont.)

Dissolve Jell-O in boiling water. Cool until mixture is syrupy. Add grapefruit and pour over firm lemon mold. Chill until ready to serve.

WHEN READY TO SERVE - Unmold on bed of lettuce or as a dessert, top each serving with a dollop of whipped cream and a sprig of mint.

CHRISTMAS SALADS

CRANBERRY SALAD

Serves 12

2	pkgs. cherry Jell-O
2	Cups water, boiling
2	tsp. lemon juice
2	cans cranberry jelly sauce
1	small can crushed pineapple
1	pint sour cream
1	Cup nuts, chopped

Dissolve Jell-O in boiling water. Stir until Jell-O is dissolved. Add remaining ingredients and stir until well mixed. Place in a lightly oiled mold, cover and refrigerate overnight.

This is wonderful with a roast turkey dinner!

CHRISTMAS SALADS

CRANBERRY AND GRAPE SALAD

Serves 8-10

1	lb. raw ground cranberries
1	Cup sugar
1	lb. seedless grapes, halved
1	pkg. miniature marshmallows
1	pint whipping cream, whipped
	English walnuts (garnish)
	Lettuce leaves (garnish)

Mix together cranberries and sugar. Add grapes and marshmallows to mixture. Fold in whipped cream. Cover and chill in refrigerator overnight, before serving.

WHEN READY TO SERVE - Serve on lettuce leaves and top with walnuts.

CHRISTMAS SALADS

LAYERED CRANBERRY SALAD

Serves 12 - 14

1	(3 oz.) pkg. vanilla pudding mix
1	(3 oz.) pkg. lemon flavored gelatin
2	Cups water
2	Tbsp. lemon juice
1	(3 oz.) pkg. raspberry flavored gelatin
1	Cup water, boiling
1	(16 oz.) can whole cranberry sauce
1/2	Cup celery, chopped
1/4	Cup pecans, chopped
1	(1.4 oz.) pkg. whipped topping mix
1/2	tsp. nutmeg
	Lettuce leaves

In a sauce pan, mix together pudding mix and lemon gelatin with 2 Cups water. Stir constantly until gelatin dissolves. Add lemon juice. Chill until consistency resembles that of a unbeaten egg white.

Dissolve raspberry gelatin in boiling water. Add cranberry sauce. Blend well. Add celery and pecans and mix well. Chill until partially set.

Prepare whipped topping mix according to package. Add nutmeg. Fold into lemon mixture. In a lightly oiled 7-cup mold, spoon in 1 1/2 cups. Chill until set.

CHRISTMAS SALADS

LAYERED CRANBERRY SALAD (cont.)

When chilled, place on top the chilled raspberry gelatin. Return to refrigerator and chill until set. Spoon remaining lemon mixture on top. Chill until firm.

WHEN READY TO SERVE - Unmold on lettuce leaves.

The layered raspberry and lemon colors nestled on a bed of green add to the setting of a festive holiday table.

CHRISTMAS SALADS

LIME PARTY SALAD

                                                                Serves 8-10

1/4	lb. marshmallows, 16 count
1	Cup milk
1	(6 oz.) pkg. lime Jell-O
2	(3 oz.) pkgs. cream cheese
1	(#2) can crushed pineapple, undrained
2/3	Cup mayonnaise
1	Cup whipping cream, (whipped)

Melt marshmallows and milk in double boiler. Add Jell-O and stir until dissolved. Add cream cheese and stir until dissolved. Add pineapple and mix well. Cool. Blend in mayonnaise. Fold in whipped cream, cover, and chill in refrigerator overnight.

Excellent salad for Christmas holiday buffet.

CHRISTMAS SALADS

CHRISTMAS SPINACH SALAD

Serves 8

2	lbs. fresh spinach
4	slices bacon, cooked and crisp
2	Tbsp. bacon drippings
1/4	Cup vinegar
1	tsp. onion, grated
1	tsp. sugar
1/2	tsp. fresh ground pepper
1	avocado, sliced
1/2	Cup pomegranate seeds

Wash spinach greens. Remove stems and towel dry spinach. Break or chop spinach leaves according to desire. Place in plastic in plastic bag and store in refrigerator until ready to use.

Saute bacon until crisp. Reserve 2 Tbsp. bacon drippings. Crumble bacon strips and set aside.

Heat together bacon drippings, vinegar, onion and sugar. To cleaned, chopped and dried spinach, add crumbled bacon and toss. Add dressing and toss. Add sliced avocado and pomegranate seeds. Serve immediately.

Christmas Main Dishes And Menus

CHRISTMAS LUNCHEON

* Raspberry Champagne Punch *

* Baked Avocado with Chicken *

* Honey Spiced Peaches *

Assorted Luncheon Rolls

* Snowballs *

Tea and Coffee

* See Index *

HOLIDAY "OPEN HOUSE" BUFFET

* Cranberry Cordial *
* Double Chocolate Egg Nog *

* Company Crab Mousse *
* Marinated Mushrooms *

* Christmas Jell-O Mold *
* Deviled Eggs *   Relish Tray

* Baked Ham with Stuffing *
* Jalapeno Jelly *   Sweet Hot Mustard
Fresh Fruit skewers
Medley of marinated vegetables

* Scones *   * Devonshire Cream *
* Sugarplums *   * Orange Sugared Walnuts *

* See Index *

CHRISTMAS "BOAT" PARADE

* Hot Buttered Rum *
* Broccoli Dip * with blanched vegetables

* Spicy Crock Pot Chili *
* Christmas Spinach Salad *
Herbed Buttered French Bread

* Pecan Tarts *
Assorted Christmas Cookies
Coffee

* See Index *

TREE TRIMMING PARTY

* Egg Nog *
* Tom and Jerry *

* Spinach Dip *   * Sherry Cheese Pate *

* Chicken Party Casserole *

Hot French Bread

Tossed Green Salad   * Pickled Beet Salad *

* Popcorn Balls *
* Gingerbread Men *

* See Index *

CHRISTMAS EVE "ENGLISH" DINNER

Cocktails

* Chicken Pate * with assorted crackers

* Star Bright Aspic *

* Prime Rib *
* Horseradish Sauce *
* Yorkshire Pudding *

* Creamed Spinach *   Broiled Tomato
Mini Parkerhouse and Potato Dinner Rolls

* Ris A La Mande *
* Fruit Cake *   * Lemon Sauce *

Coffee
* Irish Cream *

* See Index *

CHRISTMAS "MORNING" BREAKFAST

* Holiday Mimosas *
Fresh Orange Juice   Coffee and Tea

* Chili Cheese Strata *
Bacon, sausage and ham

Fresh Cut Fruit Platter

* Saint Lucia Buns *

* See Index *

CHRISTMAS "TRADITIONAL" DINNER

* Marinated Shrimp * with Cocktail Sauce
* Salmon Party Log * with assorted crackers

* Cranberry Salad *

* Roast Turkey *
* Cornbread Dressing * and Giblet Gravy

* Cranberry Sauce *   * Holiday Sauerkruat *
* Peach Potato Puffs *   Blanched green beans
* Onions Au Gratin *

* Christmas Persimmon Pudding *
Hard Sauce

* See Index *

SPECIAL HOLIDAY DINNER

Wine

Assorted Cheeses and crackers

* Layered Cranberry Salad *

* Crown Roast of Lamb * with stuffing
Mint Jelly
* Potato Souffle *   * Peas Royal *

* Almond Chocolate Cheesecake *

Coffee

See Index

CHRISTMAS MAIN DISHES

BAKED AVOCADO WITH CHICKEN

Serves 4

2	avocados
1	Cup chicken, cooked and diced
1	Cup thick cream sauce
	Grated cheese
	Butter
	Bread crumbs

Combine chicken with cream sauce. Fill each halved avocado hollow with mixture. Don't let it run over. Sprinkle with bread crumbs, cheese and dot with butter. Place in shallow baking dish and cook uncovered in moderate oven (325°) until avocados are heated through and browned on top. Serve immediately.

Nice to serve for a Christmas luncheon or bridge.

CHRISTMAS MAIN DISHES

CHICKEN PARTY CASSEROLE

Serves 6 - 8

6	chicken breasts, cooked and cubed
1	lb. noodles, cooked and drained (Cook in boiling water with 1 chopped onion and 1 tsp. salt)
1/4	lb. butter
1	pint of heavy cream
1	(3 oz.) can pimientos
1/2	Cup celery, diced
1/2	Cup green onion, chopped
1	can sliced water chestnuts
1 1/2	lbs. fresh mushrooms, sliced
1	Tbsp. poppy seed
1/2	Cup slivered almonds
1	tsp. garlic, crushed
1/2	lb. jack or cheddar cheese, grated
1	can chicken broth
1	can cream of mushroom soup
1/2	Cup white wine
1	pkg. dry dressing mix

Saute mushrooms. In a large bowl, mix butter with noodles. Add chicken and mushrooms. Excluding dressing mix, add remaining ingredients. Cover and chill in refrigerator overnight.

WHEN READY TO SERVE - Top casserole with one package of dry dressing mix. Bake at 375° uncovered for 1 hour.

Serve at your tree trimming party.

CHRISTMAS MAIN DISHES

SPICY CROCK POT CHILI

1 1/2	lbs. ground turkey
1	pkg. onion mix
1	clove garlic, minced
1	onion, chopped
1	Tbsp. basil
1	Tbsp. oregano
1	Tbsp. cumin
1	Tbsp. dried cilantro
1 1/2	Tbsp. chili powder
1	tsp. salt
1	Tbsp. pepper
4	whole cloves
2	cans red kidney beans
1	(46 oz.) can tomato juice

Break up ground turkey and place in crock pot. Add remaining ingredients and mix together. On low setting, cook for 10 hours.

SUGGESTION: Start cooking the night before.

This is great to serve on your boat at the Christmas Boat Parade.

CHRISTMAS MAIN DISHES

CHRISTMAS GOOSE

1	10 lb. goose
5	apples, peeled, cored and quartered
1/2	lb. prunes
	Salt

Parsley sprigs

Remove giblets. Rinse well and pat goose dry. Rub goose inside and out with salt. In a pan, cover prunes with water and cook until tender. Drain and remove pits. Fill goose neck and body cavities with apples and prunes. Truss goose.

In a 325° oven, place goose breast side down on a roasting rack. Using a bulb tester, periodically remove fat accumulating in bottom of pan. At the end of 3 hours, remove goose and turn breast side up. Return to oven. Bake for 1 to 2 hours or until done.

WHEN READY TO SERVE - Place goose on heated serving tray and arrange fruit stuffing around goose. Garnish with parsley.

CHRISTMAS MAIN DISHES

BAKED HAM WITH STUFFING

Serves 20

10 to 20 lb. fully cooked ham
1 1/2 Cups dried apricots, coarsely chopped
1   Cup pecans or walnuts, finely chopped
1   (8 1/2 oz.) can crushed pineapple, undrained
1/4 tsp. dried thyme leaves
1   (12 oz.) can apricot nectar
1/2 tsp. ground allspice
1/2 Cup honey

Bone ham to make cavity for stuffing. Remove 1/2 lb. of lean ham and grind.

Preheat oven to 325°. Wipe ham until dry. In bowl, mix ground ham with apricots, nuts, pineapple and thyme. Spoon into cavity.

Insert meat thermometer into thickest part of ham. Pour apricot nectar over ham. Sprinkle with allspice. Place in roasting pan and cover tightly with foil.

Bake for 2 hours. Remove foil and baste ham with half of honey. Return to oven, uncovered. Bake for 30 minutes. Baste again with remaining honey. When ready, meat thermometer should register 130. Nice Christmas dinner.

CHRISTMAS MAIN DISHES

CROWN ROAST OF LAMB

10-16 ribs of lamb
1   bottle prepared mint sauce
1   Tbsp. zest of lemon
      Juice of 1 lemon
1   tsp. olive oil
2   cloves garlic, minced
1   tsp. paprika
1   Tbsp. black pepper
1   tsp. salt

Have the butcher prepare ribs into a crown roast. In a shallow roasting pan, place rib ends up on rack. After mixing together mint sauce, lemon, garlic, oil and seasons, pour over ribs. Baste occasionally while allowing meat to come to room temperature.

When ready to roast, fill center with favorite dressing (see variation). Cover rib ends with foil. In a 450° oven bake for 20 minutes. Reduce heat to 350°. Bake for 20 to 25 minutes to the pound, basting occasionally.

WHEN READY TO SERVE - Remove foil ends and replace with cutlet frills. Garnish with parsley. Serve with mint jelly.

VARIATION - Instead of stuffing crown with dressing, bake ribs side down. When done, fill with petite peas.

CHRISTMAS MAIN DISHES

PRIME RIB ROAST

    MOTTO IS: Don't peak and don't worry. It is always perfect.

Any size   prime rib roast
               Salt and pepper to taste

Remove roast from refrigerator 2-4 hours before cooking. Preheat oven to 375°. Salt and pepper the prime rib. Place on a rack in oven, fat side up, in a shallow roasting pan. Cook uncovered for 1 hour.

TURN OVEN OFF. (DO NOT OPEN OVEN DOOR)
========================

For rare roast beef - turn oven to 300° and cook for 45 minutes before serving.

For medium roast beef - turn oven to 300° and cook for 50 minutes before serving.

For medium-well roast beef - turn oven to 300° and cook for 55 minutes before serving.

A favorite for Christmas Dinner when complimented with Yorkshire Pudding.

CHRISTMAS MAIN DISHES

ROAST LEG OF PORK

Serves 8 - 10

5-7 lb. fresh leg of pork
1   Tbsp. ground ginger
1   tsp. salt
1   tsp. pepper
1/2 Cup wine, for basting

GRAVY: 1/4 Cup port wine
            1/8 tsp. nutmeg
            1 1/2 Cups chicken broth
            2 Tbsp. flour

Rub pork with salt, pepper and ginger. In a 325° oven roast on rack uncovered for 3-4 hours (approx. 35 minutes to the lb. or until meat thermometer placed in thickest part of leg registers 170°). While roasting, baste several times with wine. During last hour of cooking remove tough skin covering pork. When cooked remove from oven and place on carving board. Cover with foil and let stand for 10-15 minutes.

For gravy, reduce pan drippings over high heat to 3 Tbsp. Stir flour into chicken broth and add wine. Add seasonings and stir into pan drippings. Bring to boil, reduce heat, while stirring to desired thickness. Add water if needed. Salt and pepper to taste.

CHRISTMAS MAIN DISHES

HOLIDAY TURKEY

Serves 10 - 20

1	10 to 20 lb. turkey
	celery tops from 1 head, chopped
1	onion, quartered
	Salt
	Sage

BASTE:

1	cube butter, melted
1	Tbsp. paprika

Remove giblets from turkey. Place giblets and turkey neck in sauce pan. Add celery tops and onion. Cover generously with water. Simmer for 1 hour or until meat falls off neck. Remove from stove and strain. Store giblets' stock in refrigerator in order to draw fat to surface. Chop giblets and neck meat finely and set aside for gravy.

Wash turkey inside and out. Pat dry. Tuck back wing tips. Rub inside of turkey with salt and sage. Fill with favorite dressing, truss and bake.

Breast side up, place turkey on rack in roasting pan. Base baking time to be 20 minutes to the pound. For first 20 minutes, bake uncovered in 400° oven. Lower oven to 325°. Baste turkey with

CHRISTMAS MAIN DISHES

HOLIDAY TURKEY (cont.)

butter and paprika. Cover completely with aluminium wrap. Return to oven for allotted time. Baste every 45 minutes and periodically with tester bulb, draw off and reserve drippings on bottom of pan. Add accumulated drippings to refrigerated giblets water. At end of allotted roasting time, remove turkey from oven. Place on serving tray, cover and allow to sit for 20 minutes before carving.

GRAVY:

        Giblets' stock and drippings
        Giblets and neck meat, finely chopped
2   Tbsp. cornstarch
2   Cups water
1   bunch parsley, minced
      Salt and pepper to taste

Discard surfaced fat from reserved giblets' stock and turkey pan drippings. Over high heat, in a large skillet, bring reserved liquid to a near boil. Gradually add water and cornstarch and stir until you have desired thickness. Add giblets and parsley. Add salt and pepper to taste. Serve immediately.

CHRISTMAS MAIN DISHES

TURKEY CURRY

>Serves 4

1/4 Cup onions, chopped
1 Tbsp. butter
1 can cream of mushroom soup
1/4 Cup milk
1 Cup sour cream
1/2 tsp. curry powder
1 Cup cooked turkey, cubed
  Salt and pepper to taste

1 1/2 Cups rice, cooked
4 parsley sprigs

Melt butter and cook onions until clear. Add soup and milk. Heat and stir until smooth. Add sour cream, curry powder and turkey. Salt and pepper to taste. Remove from heat when hot. Serve over prepared rice or store in refrigerator overnight for next day's use.

GARNISH with parsley.

VARIATION: Serve over biscuits or pasta.

CHRISTMAS MAIN DISHES

TURKEY SPAGHETTI

Serves 8 -10

4	Cups turkey, cooked and cubed
3	Cups spaghetti, broken into 2" pieces
1/2	Cup pimientos, diced
1/2	Cup green pepper, diced
2	cans cream of mushroom soup
1	Cup chicken or turkey broth
1/4	tsp. celery salt
1/4	tsp. pepper
1	medium onion, grated
3	Cups sharp cheddar cheese, grated

Cook spaghetti until barely done. Drain. Reserving 1/2 cup grated cheese for topping, mix spaghetti with all ingredients. Place mixture into a 2-quart buttered casserole. Bake covered at 350° for 45 minutes. Remove cover and top with remaining cheese. Return to oven uncovered and bake for 5 to 10 minutes, or until browned.

WHEN READY TO SERVE - Serve with a large tossed green salad and hot french bread.

A delicious late night New Year's Eve supper.

CHRISTMAS MAIN DISHES

TOURTIERE (Pork Pie)

This is a popular French Canadian Christmas dish.

1	pie shell, unbaked including enough dough for cover
1 1/2	lb. ground pork
1/2	lb. ground beef
1	onion, chopped
2	potatoes, peeled, boiled and mashed with a fork
2	Tbsp. allspice
	Salt and pepper, to taste

In a lightly salted, hot skillet, add pork and beef. Cook until meats are browned and crumbly. Pour off fat. In the same skillet, add onions and potatoes. Cook potatoes until done. Remove from stove. Drain. Mash potatoes with a fork. Add allspice, salt and pepper. Mix to correct consistency.

Place mixture into an unbaked pie shell. Roll extra dough and cover pie. Decorate top with slits from knife point. Place on middle oven rack, bake for 15 minutes at 450°. Reduce heat to 325°, and re-set pie to lower oven rack. Bake for 40 minutes, or until top is golden brown. Serve with a hot mustard sauce.

MAMA COOKS FOR CHRISTMAS

Notes ......

Christmas Side Dishes and Stuffing

CHRISTMAS SIDE DISHES & STUFFING

CRANBERRY SAUCE

1	Cup sugar
1	Cup water
1	pkg. cranberries
1/3	Cup orange marmalade
1/3	Cup almonds, slivered
1/3	Cup Armaretto

In a sauce pan, mix sugar and water together until dissolved. Bring to a boil. Add cranberries. Return to boil. Reduce heat and gently boil for 10 minutes. Remove from heat. Add marmalade and cool at room temperature.

WHEN READY TO SERVE - Add almonds and Armaretto. Place in a pretty bowl and serve.

CHRISTMAS SIDE DISHES & STUFFING

DEVONSHIRE CREAM SAUCE

1	pint whipping cream
1	Cup sour cream
1/2	Cup powdered sugar
2 oz.	Grand Marnier or Apry (apricot liqueur)

Whip heavy cream until just thickened. Slowly fold in sour cream. Continue whipping until smooth. Stir in sugar and liqueur.

WHEN READY TO SERVE: Spread over scones and serve immediately.

CHRISTMAS SIDE DISHES & STUFFING

HORSERADISH SAUCE

1/2   pint whipping cream
3   Tbsp. horseradish
1/4   tsp. salt

In a blender, whip whipping cream. Add horseradish and salt and blend until smooth and creamy.

CHRISTMAS SIDE DISHES & STUFFING

JALAPENO JELLY

Makes 6-8 sm. jars

- 1/2 Cup fresh lemon juice
- 1 Cup white vinegar
- 2 Cups green bell pepper, cored and seeded
- 1/2 Cup yellow hot chili peppers or 1 can Jalapenos
- 1/4 medium onion
- 4 1/2 Cups sugar
- 1 (6 oz.) bottle of Certo
- 8 drops green food coloring
- 1 pkg. cream cheese

Remove stems and seeds from Jalapenos. Rinse well before placing in blender with lemon juice, vinegar, green peppers and onion. Mix at high speed until well blended. In a large pan, pour mixture over sugar and mix together. Boil rapidly for 5 minutes. Reduce heat, add Certo and continue cooking for 2 more minutes. Skim off foam formed on top before adding green food coloring.

Pour jelly into sterile glass jars and seal immediately with paraffin. Let cool and refrigerate overnight.

WHEN READY TO SERVE - Spread over cream cheese and serve with crackers.

Jalapeno jelly is a lovely holiday gift.

CHRISTMAS SIDE DISHES & STUFFING

LEMON CURD

Yield: 1 quart

8	ozs. sugar
4	eggs
	Juice of 4 lemons
	Grated rind of 2 lemons
4	ozs. sweet butter, cut into pieces

Whisk eggs and sugar together. Add lemon juice, lemon rind and butter. Cook in double boiler, stirring from time to time until curd thickens - about 20-30 minutes.

Pour thickened curd into hot sterilized jars. Cover and seal while hot. Let cool overnight. Should be eaten within one month.

This is a traditional English Christmas treat.

VARIATION - Substitute lime juice for lemon juice for a delicious Lime Curd.

CHRISTMAS SIDE DISHES & STUFFING

BAKED ORANGES

4 - 5 Navel oranges

1   Cup sugar
1/2   Cup orange juice
2   Tbsp. corn syrup
6 - 8 Drops red food coloring

Cover whole oranges with cold water and boil for 45 minutes. Remove from heat and chill for 30 minutes. Peel and section oranges into slices.

In a mixing bowl, combine, sugar, orange juice, corn syrup and food coloring. Add cooled oranges. Gently coat each side of the orange slices. Arrange in a shallow greased baking dish. Bake at 325° for 45 minutes.

Delicious when served with fowl or pork.

CHRISTMAS SIDE DISHES & STUFFING

HONEY SPICED PEACHES

Serves 6 - 8

1	(1 lb. 13 oz.) can peach halves or slices, reserve liquid
1/2	Cup honey
1	stick cinnamon
12	whole cloves

Place drained peaches into mixing bowl. Set aside.

Pour reserved peach syrup into a saucepan. Add remaining ingredients and bring to boil. Simmer for 15 to 20 minutes. Strain liquid and pour over peaches. Cover and place in refrigerator overnight.

VARIATION - For a dessert, serve over vanilla ice cream or lemon sherbet.

CHRISTMAS SIDE DISHES & STUFFING

PEACH POTATO PUFFS

Serves 4-6

4	sweet potatoes
2	Tbsp. butter
2	Tbsp. sour cream
2	Tbsp. brown sugar
1/3	Cup raisins, chopped
1	tsp. lemon juice
3/4	tsp. lemon peel, grated
1/8	tsp. ground cloves
1/2	tsp. salt
1	can peach halves, drained

Drain peach halves on paper towel.

Bake sweet potatoes for 1 hour at 400 degrees. Cut potatoes in half. Scoop sweet potato in mixing bowl. Add butter and brown sugar. Add sour cream. Whip until fluffy. Add raisins, lemon juice, peel, cloves and salt. Mix well.

Arrange drained peach halves in a greased baking dish. Pile centers with potato mixture. Dot with additional butter and bake in 400° oven for 20 minutes.

VARIATION: Substitute pear halves for peach halves.

CHRISTMAS SIDE DISHES & STUFFING

PEPPER RELISH

12	green peppers, seeded and sliced
12	red peppers, seeded and sliced
12	onions, chopped
1	bunch celery, chopped
3	pints to 1 qt. vinegar
1 1/2	to 2 Cups sugar
3	Tbsp. salt
1/3	tsp. allspice

In a saucepan, cover vegetables with boiling water. Let stand for 10 minutes. Drain. Add, vinegar and sugar and boil for 15 minutes. Remove from heat and add salt and allspice.

Fill sterilized jars and seal.

A decorative holiday hostess gift.

CHRISTMAS SIDE DISHES & STUFFING

CORN BREAD STUFFING

1	pkg. corn bread mix, made according to package directions
1	lb. bacon
2	onions, chopped finely
1	bunch celery, finely chopped including tops
1	box seasoned dressing mix
1	bunch parsley, finely chopped
2	cans sliced water chestnuts
2	Tbsp. sage
2	Tbsp. poultry seasoning
1	Tbsp. black pepper
2	tsp. salt

Make corn bread according to package. Set aside. Cut raw bacon into small pieces. In a large skillet saute bacon, celery and onions until onions are clear. Add water chestnuts including liquid. Add seasonings. Cook until bacon looks to be cooked through. Remove from stove.

In a large soup kettle, break up baked corn bread. Add prepared dressing mix. Add bacon/vegetable mixture. Add parsley. Mix together well. Adjust seasonings. The dressing will not be wet and should form a soft ball when pressed together. Store overnight in the refrigerator in a large plastic bag.

Loosely stuff turkey before roasting.

CHRISTMAS SIDE DISHES & STUFFING

FRUIT STUFFING
For cornish hens

Serves 4 - 6

1/3	onion, chopped
1/3	Cup celery, chopped
1	Tbsp. butter or margarine
1	(16 oz.) can whole cranberry sauce
1/2	Cup rice, cooked
1	(8 oz.) can crushed pineapple, drained
1	(8 oz.) can apricots, drained and chopped
1	(5 oz.) can water chestnuts, drained and chopped and chopped
1/4	tsp. ground ginger
4	Tbsp. soy sauce

Saute onion and celery until onions are clear. Remove from heat and add remaining ingredients, excluding soy sauce. Spoon mixture lightly into cornish hens. Truss legs and place in a shallow baking pan. Cover with foil. Bake in 375° oven for 30 minutes. Uncover and bake for another hour. During last 30 minutes of baking, baste with soy sauce until golden brown.

Extra stuffing can be baked in a small covered casserole for 45 minutes.

CHRISTMAS SIDE DISHES & STUFFING

OYSTER STUFFING

6	Tbsp. butter, melted
1	Tbsp. parsley, chopped
1/4	Cup onion, chopped
4 - 6	Cups prepared dressing mix
1	Cup (1/2 pint) oysters, drained and chopped
3/4	tsp. salt
1/4	tsp. paprika
2	Tbsp. capers
1/2	Cup chopped spinach, drained
1/2	Cup celery, chopped
1	Cup water chestnuts, chopped

Saute onion in melted butter. Add parsley. Add all other ingredients and mix lightly. Stuff your turkey.

VARIATION - Add 1/2 lb. sliced mushrooms, 1 cup chopped giblets, 1/2 lb. chopped, cooked bacon and/or 2 Tbsp. grated lemon rind.

CHRISTMAS SIDE DISHES & STUFFING

RICE STUFFING
For a 16 lb. turkey

	Giblets and neck from turkey, cooked, shredded and chopped (Save and add water to giblets broth to make 4 Cups)
1/2	lb. sausage or hamburger
2	stalks celery, chopped
2	carrots, grated
1	medium onion, chopped
1/4	Cup fresh mushrooms, sliced
1/4	Cup water chestnuts, sliced
1	tsp. sage
1	tsp. salt
1	Tbsp. ground pepper
1	tsp. poultry seasoning
2	Cups white long grain rice
1/2	Cup slivered almonds
3	eggs, beaten

In a skillet, brown sausage until crumbly. Add shredded turkey and chopped giblets. Gradually add vegetables and seasonings. Cook until vegetables are tender.

In a saucepan, bring giblets broth to boil. Add rice and meat mixture. Cover and steam over low heat for 18 minutes, or until rice is almost tender. Remove from heat. Fold beaten eggs into dressing. Gently stir in almonds. Stuff turkey loosely and roast.

CHRISTMAS SIDE DISHES & STUFFING

RICE 'N' CASHEW STUFFING

2	(6 1/2 oz.) bags of Mrs. Cubbison's Corn Bread Stuffin'
1	Cup quick brown rice, cooked
1	Cup butter or margarine, melted
1	Cup cashews, broken
1/2	Cup celery, diced
2	Tbsp. chives, chopped
1 1/4	Cup chicken broth

Parsley sprigs
Whole cashews

Combine stuffing and rice. Add butter. Mix well. While gradually adding broth, add remaining ingredients.

Fill greased muffin cups with dressing. Bake at 350° for 20 to 25 minutes, or until golden brown.

WHEN READY TO SERVE - Garnish with parsley and a whole cashew on top.

CHRISTMAS SIDE DISHES & STUFFING

SAUSAGE/NUT DRESSING

1/4	Cup butter
1	large onion, chopped
3	stalks celery, chopped
6	Cups soft bread crumbs
1	Cup walnuts or pecans, chopped
1	lb. sausage
2	eggs, well beaten
1/4	Cup parsley, chopped
1	large apple, chopped
	Salt and pepper to taste

Saute in a large skillet, butter with onions and celery. When onions are clear, transfer cooked vegetables to another bowl. In the same skillet, add sausage. Cook sausage until brown. Add onions and celery. Mix well. Add remaining ingredients. Lightly stuff turkey when ready to roast.

CHRISTMAS SIDE DISHES & STUFFING

YORKSHIRE PUDDING

Have all ingredients at room temperature.

Serves 6

1	Cup all-purpose flour, sifted
1/2	tsp. salt
1	Cup milk
2	eggs
1/4	Cup beef drippings

Sift flour and salt together. Gradually add milk, beating until smooth after each addition. Add whole eggs, one at a time. Beat well. Chill in refrigerator for 2 hours.

Thirty minutes before serving, pour hot beef drippings into a shallow pan. Spoon chilled mixture on top. Bake at 425° for 25 to 30 minutes. Cut into squares and serve immediately.

Christmas Vegetables

CHRISTMAS VEGETABLES

ASPARAGUS SOUFFLE

Serves 6

1	(10 oz.) can asparagus soup
3/4	Cup sharp Cheddar cheese, grated
4	egg yolks, well beaten
4	egg whites, well beaten (soft peaks)

Heat soup and cheese over hot water. Stir until cheese melts. Remove from heat. In a bowl add a little soup mixture to egg yolks and add to soup mixture. Fold in egg whites. Place in a 1 1/2 quart buttered casserole. Cook in a shallow pan of water in 300° oven for 1 hour. This souffle is very durable.

CHRISTMAS VEGETABLES

BROCCOLI CASSEROLE

Serves 6

2	(10 oz.) pkgs. frozen chopped broccoli, cooked and drained
2	eggs, beaten
1	Cup mayonnaise
1	can cream of mushroom soup
1	Cup sharp Cheddar cheese, grated
	Potato chips

Excluding potato chips, mix ingredients together. Pour mixture into a buttered (13"x9") casserole. Cover and refrigerate overnight.

WHEN READY TO SERVE - Bake for 25 minutes in 350° oven. Remove from oven, top with crushed potato chips and return to oven for 10 minutes to brown the top.

CHRISTMAS VEGETABLES

GREEN BEAN CASSEROLE

Serves 8

2	(10 oz.) pkgs. frozen green beans, French cut - thawed and dry
1	onion, chopped
1	can bean sprouts, drained
1	can water chestnuts, drained and sliced
1	can cream of mushroom soup
1	Mozzarella ball, grated
1	can onion rings, French fried

Saute green beans and onion. Excluding onion rings, add remaining ingredients and mix well. Top with onion rings. Pour into a buttered casserole, cover and refrigerate overnight.

WHEN READY TO SERVE - Bake for 30 minutes at 350° or until browned.

CHRISTMAS VEGETABLES

PARTY GREEN BEANS

Serves 6 - 8

2   cans cut green beans, drained
2   (4 oz.) cans mushrooms, drained
1   can tomatoes, undrained
1   onion, chopped
1/2   Cup maple syrup
8 - 10 slices of raw bacon, cut into 1"
        pieces

In a casserole, place all ingredients. Mix together. Place in a 325° oven for 2 hours. Serve immediately.

CHRISTMAS VEGETABLES

ONIONS AU GRATIN

Serves 5 - 6

2	lbs.	whole small fresh onions, peeled and par-boiled
2	Tbsp.	butter or margarine, melted
3	Tbsp.	cheddar cheese, grated
3	Tbsp.	bread crumbs
1/4	tsp.	salt

Preheat oven to 400°. Place par-boiled onions in a buttered baking dish. Pour butter over onions. Combine cheese, bread crumbs and salt. Sprinkle on top of onions. Bake for 10 to 15 minutes in 350 oven, or until browned slightly on top.

CHRISTMAS VEGETABLES

PEAS ROYAL

Serves 3 - 4

3	slices bacon, cooked & crisp
1	(2 oz.) can slice mushrooms, drained
	Juice of 1/2 lemon
1	Tbsp. sugar
2	tsp. instant minced onion
1/2	tsp. salt
1	(10 oz.) pkg. frozen petit peas cooked and drained

Crumble bacon slices. In a sauce pan, combine bacon, mushrooms, lemon juice, sugar, instant onion, salt and petit peas. Cook until hot. Serve immediately.

CHRISTMAS VEGETABLES

POTATO SOUFFLE

Serves 6

2	Cups mashed potatoes
1	(8 oz.) pkg. cream cheese
1	(8 oz.) carton sour cream
2	eggs
1/2	Cup Milk
1	small onion, diced
2	Tbsp. flour
	Salt and pepper to taste
1	(3 1/2 oz.) can French fried onions

In a large bowl, mash potatoes. Add milk and mix well. Add softened cheese, sour cream, eggs, onion and flour. Beat at low speed until blended, then at high speed until fluffy and light. Add salt and pepper to taste. In a buttered round 9" baking dish place potato mixture. Cover and refrigerate overnight.

WHEN READY TO SERVE - Sprinkle with fried onions and bake in a moderate oven for 35-40 minutes until hot and browned on top.

CHRISTMAS VEGETABLES

WILD RICE CASSEROLE

Serves 6 - 8

1/4	Cup margarine
1	Cup celery, thinly sliced
1/2	Cup onion, chopped
7	oz. wild rice
3	packets chicken flavored instant broth
3	Cups water
1/4	tsp. salt
1/8	tsp. pepper

In skillet, saute celery and onion in margarine. Cook until tender. Remove from heat. Add wild rice and pour into an ungreased 1 1/2 quart casserole.

In the same skillet, bring to boil, broth, water, salt and pepper. Pour liquid over rice mixture in casserole. Cover and bake at 350° for 1 hour and 20 minutes, or until liquid is absorbed.

CHRISTMAS VEGETABLES

HOLIDAY SAUERKRAUT

A Czechoslovakian tradition with turkey

1	(29 oz.) can sauerkraut, drained
1	large onion, chopped
1	Tbsp. caraway seeds
1	Tbsp. dill weed

Place sauerkraut in a saucepan, cover with water. Add onion, caraway seed and dill. Cook until onions are opaque. Simmer, and add drippings as you baste your turkey.

WHEN READY TO SERVE - Top with gravy and serve hot.

This side dish is a tradition in our family. We always serve it with holiday turkey.

CHRISTMAS VEGETABLES

CREAMED SPINACH

Serves 4

1	lb. fresh spinach or
	1 box frozen chopped spinach
3 - 4	strips bacon, finely chopped
1	clove garlic, chopped fine
1	medium onion
2	Tbsp. butter
2	Tbsp. flour
1	Cup milk
	Salt and pepper to taste

Cook spinach until barely done. Drain and squeeze dry. (When using fresh spinach, chop finely when cooked.) Saute chopped bacon and onion. Add garlic, salt and pepper. Add spinach and saute until all moisture is gone.

In a sauce pan, make a medium cream sauce with butter, flour and milk. Add to seasoned spinach and bring to a slow boil. Serve immediately.

CHRISTMAS VEGETABLES

BERRY MALLOW YAM BAKE

Serves 6 - 8

1/2	Cup flour
1/2	Cup brown sugar
1/2	Cup old fashioned or quick oats, uncooked
1	tsp. cinnamon
1/3	Cup margarine, cold
2	cans (17 oz.) yams, drained and sliced
2	Cups fresh cranberries, raw
1 1/2	Cups miniature marshmallows

Cut margarine into flour, sugar, oats and cinnamon until it resembles coarse crumbs. With 1 cup of coarse crumbs add yams and cranberries. Place in a buttered 1 1/2 quart casserole. Top with remaining coarse crumbs. Cover and refrigerate overnight.

WHEN READY TO SERVE - Top casserole with 1 1/2 Cups miniature marshmallows. Bake at 350° until brown on top and bubbly hot.

CHRISTMAS VEGETABLES

YAM BALLS

4	medium yams or 2 medium. cans sweet potatoes, drained
1/2	tsp. salt
1/2	tsp. cinnamon
1/4	tsp. nutmeg
1/4	tsp. ginger
	Pecans, finely chopped

Mix all ingredients together and form into small balls. Roll in chopped nuts. Place on a greased cookie sheet and bake for 20 minutes in a 350° oven.

CHRISTMAS VEGETABLES

ZUCCHINI CHEESE CASSEROLE

Serves 8 - 10

4 -5	large zucchini, grated
1/2	lb. Cheddar cheese, grated
1	onion, grated
1	stack of Ritz crackers, crushed
6	eggs, beaten
	Salt and pepper to taste
	Parmesan cheese, grated

Mix together crackers, eggs, salt and pepper. Add cheese and zucchini and mix well. Pour into a buttered casserole. Top with Parmesan cheese. Cover and refrigerate overnight.

WHEN READY TO SERVE - Bake for 3/4 to 1 hour at 350° or until browned and egg has set.

CHRISTMAS VEGETABLES

STUFFED ZUCCHINI

Serves 6

6	small/medium zucchini
2	Cups soft bread crumbs
2	Tbsp. butter, melted
1/2	Cup salami, finely chopped
1	egg, slightly beaten
1	Tbsp. water
1/4	onion, chopped
1	Tbsp. parsley, chopped
1/2	Tbsp. poultry seasoning
1/4	tsp. salt
1/8	tsp. pepper
1/4	Cup Parmesan cheese, grated

Cut zucchini in half, lengthwise. Scoop out seeded area. Blanch zucchini, drain and set aside. Excluding cheese, mix together the above ingredients. Fill each zucchini with breaded mixture. Dot with butter and sprinkle cheese on top and place in greased casserole. Cover and refrigerate overnight.

WHEN READY TO SERVE - Bake for 25-30 minutes in 375° oven.

VARIATION - Substitute chopped cooked turkey for salami.

This is a delicious side dish to serve with meat and salad.

Christmas Desserts

CHRISTMAS DESSERTS

OLD FASHIONED CARROT PUDDING

Serves 6 - 8

1	Cup seedless, raisins, rinsed and drained
1	Cup sugar
1	Cup all-purpose flour, sifted
1	tsp. soda
1/2	tsp. salt
1/2	tsp. cinnamon
1/2	tsp. nutmeg
1/2	tsp. ground cloves
2	Tbsp. butter, melted
1	Cup raw carrot, grated
1	Cup raw potato, grated

Sift dry ingredients together. Add raisins and stir until coated. Combine butter with carrot and potato. Blend thoroughly with dry ingredients. Pour into a well greased one-pound coffee can or 2 #303 tin cans. Cover end with foil and tie with string. Place tins into cooking pot with boiling water rising to half the depth of the cans. Cover. Bring water to a boil and keep boiling. If using coffee can boil for 2 hours. If using #303 can, boil for 1 hour.

This is excellent hot or cold served with a Lemon Sauce. Any extra will freeze well.

CHRISTMAS DESSERTS

LEMON SAUCE

1/2	Cup sugar
1	Tbsp. cornstarch
1	Cup boiling water
	Salt
2	Tbsp. butter
2	Tbsp. lemon juice
	Nutmeg

In top of a double boiler, combine sugar and cornstarch. Add boiling water and a pinch of salt. Boil until mixture is thick and clear.

Place top of double boiler over boiling water and continue cooking for 20 minutes. Beat in butter, lemon juice and a pinch of nutmeg. Serve warm.

VARIATION - This sauce is wonderful served over plum pudding or fruit cake. A delicious sauce!

CHRISTMAS DESSERTS

ALMOND CHOCOLATE CHEESECAKE

Serves 12 - 16

CRUST:
- 1 (8 1/2 oz.) pkg. chocolate wafers, finely crushed (approximately. 2 1/2 cups)
- 1/2 Cup butter or margarine, melted

Combine cookie crumbs and butter. Mix well. Press into a 9" spring form pan going up sides 2" all around. Place in refrigerator.

FILLING:
- 3 (8 oz.) pkgs. cream cheese, softened
- 3/4 Cup sugar
- 4 eggs
- 1 (6 oz.) pkg. milk chocolate chips, melted
- 1 Cup sour cream
- 1/2 Cup Amaretto liqueur
- 4 Tbsp. butter or margarine, melted
- 1 tsp. vanilla

Beat cream cheese and sugar until fluffy. Add eggs, one at a time and beat well after each addition. Blend in chocolate. Add sour cream, liqueur, butter and vanilla. Mix well. Pour into prepared crust. Bake in 350° oven for 1 hour or until just set. Remove from oven.

CHRISTMAS DESSERTS

ALMOND CHOCOLATE CHEESECAKE (cont.)

TOPPING: 1   Cup sour cream
          2   Tbsp. Amaretto liqueur
               Toasted sliced almonds

Mix together sour cream and liqueur.

Spread sour cream mixture over top of cheesecake and return to oven for 3 to 5 minutes. Remove from oven. Cool. Cover and chill. Garnish with sliced almonds.

CHRISTMAS DESSERTS

CHRISTMAS FRUIT CAKE

Makes 4 large loaves or 16 mini loaves

1	lb.	butter
1	dozen	eggs
1	lb.	brown sugar
1	Cup	honey
1/2	Cup	brandy
1	Cup	jelly
1	lb.	walnuts
1	lb.	pecans
1	lb.	almonds
1	lb.	Brazil nuts
1	lb.	seeded raisins
1/2	lb.	small gum drops
3	lbs.	candied fruit
1	lb.	candied pineapple
3 1/5	Cups	flour

Brandy

Cream butter and sugar, beat in whole eggs. Add honey, brandy and jelly. Beat until smooth. Toss together flour, fruit, nuts and gum drops. Add to butter and sugar mixture and blend well.

Line loaf pans with brown paper and pour in mixture. Bake for 3 1/2 to 4 hours in a slow oven, 325°.

CHRISTMAS DESSERTS

CHRISTMAS FRUIT CAKE (cont.)

When cool, turn out of pans. Wrap each fruit cake in cheese cloth. Place in a covered pan to allow to age in a dark area. Every month, uncover and pour a small amount of brandy over the cakes. Re-wrap to allow to age some more.

When ready to give as a gift, wrap in bright Christmas foil and tie with a lovely ribbon. A wonderful Christmas hostess gift.

CHRISTMAS DESSERTS

CHESS TARTS

Serves 8

1   cube butter, softened
1   (3 oz.) pkg. cream cheese
1   Cup flour

Using a fork, Mix butter and cream cheese together. Add flour and mix well, until it forms a ball. Make a walnut size ball and press into shape in a tart pan. Keep cool and set aside.

FILLING: 2   Cups sugar
            1   Cup butter
            4   eggs, separated
            3   Tbsp. vinegar
            1/2   tsp. vanilla
            1/2   tsp. cinnamon
            1/2   tsp. allspice
            1/2   tsp. cloves
            1   Cup nuts
            1   Cup raisins

Cream together sugar and butter. Before adding to mixture, combine vinegar and egg yolks and beat well. Add seasonings and mix well. Add nuts and raisins. Fold in stiffly beaten egg whites. Place mixture into tart pans. Bake in a slow oven for about 1 hour. When cooled, cover and place in refrigerator overnight.

CHRISTMAS DESSERTS

CREME DE MENTHE TORTE

90-95 marshmallows
3/4 Cup green Creme de Menthe
2 pints whipping cream, whipped
22 lady fingers
1 box chocolate wafers
   chocolate scrolls

Over low heat, melt marshmallows with Creme de Menthe. Do not allow to boil. Remove from heat. Set aside.

Whip cream until it mounds lightly. Not stiff! Set aside 2 cups for topping. Over remainder, pour marshmallow mixture on top. Stir until equally distributed.

In a buttered and sugared 9" springform pan, arrange chocolate wafers on bottom. Arrange lady fingers around sides. Pour in mixture. Spread reserved whipped cream on top. Garnish with chocolate scrolls. Cover with plastic wrap and refrigerate overnight.

CHRISTMAS DESSERTS

WINE-PECAN CAKE

So easy to make, yet so good!

1	box yellow cake mix
1	regular size box instant vanilla pudding mix
1/2	Cup oil
4	eggs
3/4	Cup sherry
1/4	Cup water
1	Cup pecans, chopped

Excluding nuts, mix together all ingredients. Beat until well blended. Add nuts. Bake in a greased bundt pan for 1 hour at 350°.

VARIATION - This recipe can also be baked in 2 greased loaf pans for 45 minutes at 350.

CHRISTMAS DESSERTS

PECAN TARTS

Makes 24 miniature tarts

CRUST:
- 1 cube butter
- 1 (3 oz.) pkg. cream cheese
- 1 Cup flour

Using a fork, mix together butter and cream cheese. Gradually add flour. Stir mixture until a ball forms. Using your fingers, press mixture into miniature muffin tins.

FILLING:
- 2 eggs, beaten
- 2 Cups brown sugar
- 1 tsp. vanilla
- Dash of salt
- 1 Cup pecans, finely chopped

Excluding pecans, mix all ingredients together. (Do not over-mix.) Into each muffin tin, place 1 tsp. pecans. Pour in filling to be about 3/4's full. Top with a few more pecans. Bake for 15-20 in a 350° oven. Let set for a few minutes before removing from tins.

CHRISTMAS DESSERTS

PEPPERMINT WAFER DESSERT

Serves 8 - 10

1/2	lb. peppermint stick candy, crushed
1/2	Cup light cream
1/2	Tbsp. unflavored gelatin, (1/2 of an envelope)
2	Tbsp. cold water
1 1/2	Cups whipping cream, whipped
1	(10 oz.) can chocolate wafers

In a double boiler, mix together crushed candy and light cream. Stir until candy dissolves. Soften gelatin in cold water. Add to candy mixture. Remove from stove and chill until partially set. Fold in whipped cream.

Break in half enough wafers to set around outside of greased 9" square pan. Place a layer of whole wafers on bottom of pan. Spread one half of the candy mixture on top of wafers. Add a layer of wafers. Spread candy mixture on top. Finish with a layer of wafers. Chill overnight.

WHEN READY TO SERVE - Cut into squares.

CHRISTMAS DESSERTS

CHRISTMAS PERSIMMON PUDDING

1	Cup sugar
1	Tbsp. butter, melted
1/2	Cup milk
2	tsp. baking soda
2	persimmons, chopped pulp
1	Cup flour
1 1/2	tsp. baking powder
	Pinch of salt

Cream sugar with butter. Combine milk and soda. Add mixture to creamed butter. Add persimmon pulp. Gradually add flour and mix well. Add baking powder and salt. Beat until smooth. Pour into an oiled mold. Steam over boiling water for 2 hours. Serve with sauce.

SAUCE:

1	Cup granulated sugar
2	Tbsp. butter, melted
1	egg yolk, separated
1/2	pint whipping cream, whipped
1	tsp. vanilla

Cream sugar with butter. Beat egg yolk and add to mixture. Add vanilla. In a small bowl, stiffly beat egg white. Stiffly beat whipping cream and fold into mixture. Fold in stiffly beaten egg white. Serve with persimmon pudding.

At Christmas, it is a tradition!

CHRISTMAS DESSERTS

PINEAPPLE AND DATE TORTE

Serves 10

1	Cup pineapple, chopped
1	Cup dates, chopped
1	Cup nuts, chopped
1/2	Cup flour
1	tsp. baking powder
1	tsp. salt
3	egg yolks, well beaten
3/4	Cup sugar
1	tsp. vanilla
3	egg whites, well beaten

Mix together pineapple, dates and nuts. Sift together flour, baking powder and salt. Mix egg yolks with sugar and toss with fruit and nut mixture. Gradually add dry ingredients. Mix well. Add vanilla. Fold in stiff egg whites.

In a shallow buttered pan bake for 30 to 35 minutes in a 325° oven.

WHEN READY TO SERVE - Top each serving of the torte with Orange Pudding Sauce.

CHRISTMAS DESSERTS

ORANGE PUDDING SAUCE

Serves 25 - 30

1	lb. powdered sugar
1/4	Cup butter
1	can frozen orange juice
2	tsp. brandy
2	tsp. vanilla
1/2	Cup whipped cream

Cream sugar and butter. Add orange juice, brandy and vanilla. Fold in whipped cream. Will keep in the refrigerator.

CHRISTMAS DESSERTS

PRISM CAKE

Serves 16 -20

1	pkg. orange gelatin
1	pkg. cherry gelatin
1	pkg. lime gelatin
3	Cups hot water
1 1/2	Cups cold water
1	Cup pineapple juice
1	pkg. lemon gelatin
1/4	Cup sugar
1/2	Cup cold water
1	Cup graham cracker crumbs
1/4	Cup butter or margarine, melted
2 1/2	Cups whipping cream, whipped

Prepare orange, cherry and lime gelatin mixes using 1 Cup hot water and 1/2 Cup cold water for each package. Pour each gelatin into a 8"x8"x2" pan and chill until set.

Mix together graham cracker crumbs and butter. Press mixture smoothly over bottom of a 9" spring form pan. Set aside.

Heat pineapple juice with sugar. Stir until sugar dissolves. Remove from heat and add lemon gelatin. Add 1/2 cup water. Stir until gelatin dissolves. Chill until syrupy.

CHRISTMAS DESSERTS

PRISM CAKE (cont.)

Add 2 cups whipped cream to syrupy lemon gelatin.

Cut firm orange, cherry and lime gelatin into 1/2" cubes. Fold into mixture. Pour into spring form pan and refrigerate overnight. When ready, remove sides of pan and frost with additional sweetened whipped cream.

CHRISTMAS DESSERTS

POPCORN CAKE

```
1 1/4  Cup un-popped popcorn
1      Cup margarine, melted
16     oz. pkg. miniature marshmallows
1      (6 1/2 oz.) can cocktail peanuts
1      lb. bag of sugar
1      bag gum drops, cut into 1/8" pieces
         (do not use black gum drops)
```

Pop the popcorn. Add butter and toss until evenly covered. Add remaining ingredients and gently mix. Put in a greased angel food cake. Pat down until firmly packed and everything sticks together. Place in refrigerator for 1 hour. Remove from cake pan and slice with a sharp knife.

Young children love to help make this and of course eat it.

CHRISTMAS DESSERTS

PUMPKIN PIE CAKE

    Wonderful at Thanksgiving too!

1   large can pumpkin
3   eggs
1   large can evaporated milk
1   Cup sugar
1   tsp. pumpkin pie spice

Mix together all ingredients and pour into a greased 9"x12" baking pan.

TOPPING: 1   pkg. yellow cake mix
                 1   cube butter or margarine, melted
                 1   Cup nuts, chopped

Sprinkle cake mix over pudding mixture. Drizzle butter on top. Top with nuts and bake for 1 hour at 325°.

VARIATION: A prepared pumpkin pie filling may be used instead of mixing the first 5 ingredients. Then, follow topping instructions.

CHRISTMAS DESSERTS

RUM PUDDING

1	envelope plain gelatin
1/4	Cup cold water
5	egg yolks, beaten
3/4	Cup sugar
1	pint milk, hot
1/2	Cup rum
1	Cup whipped cream

Soak gelatin in cold water until soft. Beat egg yolks and sugar together until frothy and lemon colored. Stirring constantly, slowly add hot milk. Pour mixture into top of double boiler, over hot water, and cook until smooth and creamy. Add gelatin mixture and blend well. Cool. Add rum and fold in whipped cream. Pour into a mold and chill for several hours.

Wonderful served with Raspberry Sauce.

CHRISTMAS DESSERTS

RASPBERRY SAUCE

1	Cup raspberry juice
3/4	Cup currant jelly
1	Tbsp. cornstarch

In a sauce pan, melt together 3/4 cup juice and jelly. When mixture has reached a boil blend in cornstarch and remainder of juice. Reduce heat to low. Stir constantly until sauce becomes clear and thickens. Cool and pass with Rum Pudding.

CHRISTMAS DESSERTS

RASPBERRY RUM MOUSSE

Serves 6 - 8

1	can raspberries
2/3	Cup water
1/3	Cup rum
1	small pkg. raspberry Jell-O
1	Cup whipping cream, whipped
16	marshmallows, cut up

Drain raspberries and retain juice. Combine 1 cup of raspberry juice, water and rum. Bring to a boil. Add marshmallows. Stir until dissolved. Stirring constantly, add Jell-O to mixture. Remove from stove. Chill until fairly well set. When thick, fold in raspberries and whipped cream. Pour mousse into a lightly oiled mold and chill overnight, covered.

CHRISTMAS DESSERTS

RIS A LA MANDE (Rice Pudding)

A delightful tradition at Christmas Eve dinner.

1/2   Cup rice, uncooked
1 1/2 Cup milk
1/2   vanilla bean
1/2   pint whipping cream, whipped
1/2   Cup almonds, chopped
1   whole blanched almond

1   can whole cherries

Boil milk and rice for 20 minutes over medium heat, stirring occasionally. Let cook until milk is absorbed. Allow porridge to cool before adding whipped cream and nuts and 1 whole almond.

WHEN READY TO SERVE - Garnish with canned cherries.

This is a wonderful tradition when served on Christmas Eve. The person finding the whole almond in their dish receives a special surprise. If a child, maybe being allowed to open one present before Santa arrives!

CHRISTMAS DESSERTS

SNOW FLAKE PUDDING

1	Cup sugar
1/2	tsp. salt
1	envelope plain gelatin
1 1/2	Cups milk
2	Cups whipped cream
1 1/2	Cups coconut flakes
1	Cup walnuts, chopped
1	tsp. vanilla

In a sauce pan, over medium heat, mix together sugar, salt, gelatin and milk. Stir until dissolved into milk. Chill until partially set. Gently mix together whipped cream, coconut, nuts and vanilla. Fold into chilled mixture. Pour into sherbert glasses.

WHEN READY TO SERVE - Serve with Raspberry sauce.

CHRISTMAS DESSERTS

RASPBERRY SAUCE

2   (10 oz.) cans frozen raspberries, thawed
3   Tbsp. cornstarch
1   Cup red currant jelly

In a sauce pan add raspberries, cornstarch and jelly. Bring to a boil. Stir until mixture is clear and thickened. Strain, cover and chill until ready to serve.

CHRISTMAS DESSERTS

SAND KAGE (Danish Cake)

1	lb. butter
2	Cups sugar
4	Cups flour
8	eggs
2	Tbsp. cocoa

Cream butter and sugar. Add eggs and flour. Beat until well mixed. Divide batter in half and add cocoa to one half of the batter.

In a greased loaf pan, put plain half of batter on bottom of pan and top with chocolate batter. Bake in a 350° oven for 1 hour.

The cake stores well and is delicious when served as a holiday dessert. Also, makes a festive gift.

CHRISTMAS DESSERTS

SNOWBALLS

Serves 12 - 16

1	Cup sugar
1/2	Cup butter
2	eggs, separated
1	Cup crushed pineapple, drained
1	Cup walnuts, finely chopped
2	pkgs. lemon wafers

Cream sugar and butter. Add slightly beaten egg yolks to mixture and beat. Add walnuts and crushed pineapple and mix well. Beat egg whites until stiff and fold into creamed mixture. Alternating wafers, place 1 tsp. filling, making a four high cookie stack. Cover and chill overnight.

WHEN READY TO SERVE - Frost with 1 pint whipping cream, whipped, and roll into tinted coconut.

This is a very nice holiday luncheon dessert.

CHRISTMAS DESSERTS

HARVEY WALLBANGER PIE

1	9" prepared pie shell, baked and cool
1	envelope unflavored gelatin
1/2	Cup sugar
1/4	tsp. salt
1/2	Cup orange juice
1/4	Cup water
2	tsp. lemon juice
3	eggs, separated
1/2	Cup Galliano liqueur
2	Tbsp. vodka
1	Cup whipping cream
2	orange slices

In a medium sauce pan, combine gelatin, sugar and salt. Slightly beat egg yolks and add to gelatin mixture. Add orange juice, water, and lemon juice. Cook over medium heat until gelatin is dissolved and slightly thickened. Remove from heat and cool slightly. Stir in liqueur and vodka. Chill until partially set. The mixture should resemble unbeaten egg whites.

Beat egg whites until soft peaks curl at top. Gradually add remaining sugar and beat until peaks are straight. Fold into partially set gelatin.

CHRISTMAS DESSERTS

HARVEY WALLBANGER PIE (cont.)

Whip cream to soft peaks. Chill until whipped cream mounds when dropped from a spoon. Fold into gelatin mixture. Turn into cooled pastry shell. Chill 4 - 5 hours. Garnish with orange slices attractively displayed on top of pie.

CHRISTMAS DESSERTS

YULE CAKE

1 1/2	Cup	whole Brazil nuts
1 1/2	Cup	walnut halves
7 1/4	oz.	pitted dates
2/3	Cup	candied mixed fruit
1/2	Cup	red maraschino cherries
1/2	Cup	green maraschino cherries
1/2	Cup	raisins
3		eggs
3/4	Cup	flour, sifted
3/4	Cup	sugar
1/2	tsp.	baking powder
1/2		salt
1	tsp.	vanilla

In a large bowl, toss nuts and fruit with flour. Add sugar, baking powder and salt and mix well. Beat eggs and vanilla together. Add to floured fruit and nut mixture. Blend well.

Spoon mixture into foil lined bread pans. Bake for 1 1/2 - 1 3/4 hours in a 300° oven. When baked remove foil and allow to cool. Re-wrap in foil and refrigerate for 24 hours before cutting.

Will keep for 2 to 3 months when stored covered in the refrigerator.

MAMA COOKS FOR CHRISTMAS

Notes ......

MAMA COOKS FOR CHRISTMAS

Notes ......

MAMA COOKS FOR CHRISTMAS

CHRISTMAS APPETIZERS:

Broccoli Dip	1
Sherry Cheese Pate	2
Chicken Pate	3
Marinated Chicken Wings	4
Company Crab Mousse	5
Deviled Eggs	6
Deviled Ham Holiday Puffs	7
Marinated Mushrooms	9
Salmon Party Log	10
Marinated Shrimp	11
Spinach Dip	12

CHRISTMAS BEVERAGES:

Cappucino	13
Cranberry Cordial	14
Double Chocolate Egg Nog	15
Old Fashioned Egg Nog	16
Christmas Spiced Glogg	17
Irish Cream	18
Kahlua	19
Holiday Mimosas	20
Christmas Punch	21
Raspberry Champagne Punch	22
Hot Buttered Rum	23
Tom and Jerry	24

CHRISTMAS BRUNCH AND BREADS:

Sauteed Apples with Noodles and Sausage	25
Christmas Cake (Jolakaka)	26
Party Coffee Cake	27

Index

MAMA COOKS FOR CHRISTMAS

CHRISTMAS BRUNCH AND BREADS: (Cont.)

Cranberry Bread	28
Hawaiian Bread	29
Sour Cream Nut Bread	30
Honey Puff Pancake	31
Swedish Pancakes	32
Pumpkin Bread	33
Herbed Spinach Quiche	34
Saint Lucia Buns	35
Scones	36
Chili-Cheese Strata	37
Zucchini Bread	38

CHRISTMAS COOKIES & CANDIES:

Almond Christmas Cookies	39
Almond Lacy Cookies	40
Almond Squares	41
Teriyaki Almonds	42
Holly Bourbon Balls	43
Butterballs	44
Candy Cane Cookies	45
Caramels	46
English Toffee	47
Grandma's Fudge	48
Gingerbread People	49
Candied Grapefruit Peel	50
Holiday Delight	51
French Lemon Squares	52
Linzertart	53
Mince Meat Miniatures	54
Peanut Brittle	55
Persimmon Cookies	56
Popcorn Balls	57

Index

MAMA COOKS FOR CHRISTMAS

CHRISTMAS COOKIES & CANDIES: (Cont.)

Rosettes	58
Santa's Cookies	59
Christmas Strawberries	60
Spritz Cookies	61
Starlight Sugar Crisps	62
Sugarplums	63
Christmas Nuts	64
Chocolate Tea Cookies	65
Special Christmas Tea Cookies	67
Truffles	68
Orange Sugared Walnuts	69
Walnut Roll	70

CHRISTMAS SALADS:

Star Bright Aspic	71
Pickled Beet Salad	73
Broccoli Salad	74
Christmas Jell-O Mold	75
Cranberry Salad	77
Cranberry and Grape Salad	78
Layered Cranberry Salad	79
Lime Party Salad	81
Christmas Spinach Salad	82

CHRISTMAS MENUS

Christmas Luncheon	83
Holiday "Open House" Buffet	84
Christmas "Boat" Parade	85
Tree Trimming Party	86
Christmas Eve "English" Dinner	87

Index

MAMA COOKS FOR CHRISTMAS

CHRISTMAS MENU'S (Cont.)

Christmas "Morning" Breakfast	88
Christmas "Traditional" Dinner	89
Special Holiday Dinner	90

CHRISTMAS MAIN DISHES:

Baked Avocado With Chicken	91
Chicken Party Casserole	92
Spicy Crock Pot Chili	93
Christmas Goose	94
Baked Ham With Stuffing	95
Crown Roast of Lamb	96
Prime Rib Roast	97
Roast Leg Of Pork	98
Holiday Turkey	99
Turkey Curry	101
Turkey Spaghetti	102
Tourtiere (Pork Pie)	103

CHRISTMAS SIDE DISHES & STUFFING:

Cranberry Sauce	105
Devonshire Cream Sauce	106
Horseradish Sauce	107
Jalapeno Jelly	108
Lemon Curd	109
Baked Oranges	110
Honey Spiced Peaches	111
Peach Potato Puffs	112
Pepper Relish	113
Corn Bread Stuffing	114
Fruit Stuffing	115

Index

MAMA COOKS FOR CHRISTMAS

CHRISTMAS SIDE DISHES & STUFFING: (Cont.)

Oyster Stuffing	116
Rice Stuffing	117
Rice 'N' Cashew Stuffing	118
Sausage/Nut Dressing	119
Yorkshire Pudding	120

CHRISTMAS VEGETABLES:

Asparagus Souffle	121
Broccoli Casserole	122
Green Bean Casserole	123
Party Green Beans	124
Onions Au Gratin	125
Peas Royal	126
Potato Souffle	127
Wild Rice Casserole	128
Holiday Sauerkraut	129
Creamed Spinach	130
Berry Mallow Yam Bake	131
Yam Balls	132
Zucchini Cheese Casserole	133
Stuffed Zucchini	134

CHRISTMAS DESSERTS:

Old Fashioned Carrot Pudding	135
Lemon Sauce	136
Almond Chocolate Cheesecake	137
Christmas Fruit Cake	139
Chess Tarts	141
Creme de Menthe Torte	142
Wine-Pecan Cake	143

Index

MAMA COOKS FOR CHRISTMAS

CHRISTMAS DESSERTS: (Cont.)

Pecan Tarts	144
Peppermint Water Dessert	145
Christmas Persimmon Pudding	146
Pineapple & Date Torte	147
Orange Pudding Sauce	148
Prism Cake	149
Popcorn Cake	151
Pumpkin Pie Cake	152
Rum Pudding	153
Raspberry Sauce	154
Raspberry Rum Mousse	155
Ris A La Mande	156
Snow Flake Pudding	157
Raspberry Sauce	158
Sand Kage	159
Snowballs	160
Harvey Wallbanger Pie	161
Yule Log	163

Index

Merry Christmas to All!

Mail to: MAMA COOKS FOR CHRISTMAS
P.O. Box 7991, Newport Beach, CA 92658

Please send _____ books. Price per copy: $7.95 + $2.00 postage/handling & California residents add .0775% sales tax. (For your convenience: California residents total, $10.56 per copy and out-of-state residents, $9.95 per copy.) Thank you, Toni & Bette.

Name _____

Address _____

City _____ State _____ Zip ___

===

Mail to: MAMA COOKS FOR CHRISTMAS
P.O. Box 7991, Newport Beach, CA 92658

Please send _____ books. Price per copy: $7.95 + $2.00 postage/handling & California residents add .0775% sales tax. (For your convenience: California residents total, $10.56 per copy and out-of-state residents, $9.95 per copy.) Thank you, Toni & Bette.

Name _____

Address _____

City _____ State _____ Zip ___